DEALING WITH DIFFICULT PARENTS

(AND WITH PARENTS IN DIFFICULT SITUATIONS)

Todd Whitaker
Douglas J. Fiore

Routledge
Taylor & Francis Group
New York London

ABOUT THE AUTHORS

Dr. Todd Whitaker is an Associate Professor of Educational Leadership at Indiana State University in Terre Haute, Indiana. Prior to coming to Indiana, he taught at the junior high and high school level in Missouri. Following his teaching experience, he served as a middle and high school principal for eight years. In addition, Dr. Whitaker served as middle school coordinator in Jefferson City for two new middle schools.

Dr. Whitaker has been published in the areas of principal effectiveness, teacher leadership, change, staff motivation, and middle level practices. His previous books include *Dealing With Difficult Teachers* and *Motivating & Inspiring Teachers—The Educational Leaders Guide For Building Staff Morale*. He is a highly sought speaker for teachers and principals. He has made over 500 presentations including state, national, and international presentations.

Todd is married to Beth, a former teacher and principal, who is an assistant professor of elementary education at Indiana State. They are coeditors of *Contemporary Education*, an international educational journal. Beth and Todd have three children, Katherine, 11; Madeline, 9; and Harrison, 2.

Dr. Douglas J. Fiore is currently the Assistant Dean of the College of Education at the State University of West Georgia. Prior to coming to Georgia, he taught at the elementary school level in Indiana. Following his teaching experience, he served as an elementary school principal in two Indiana schools.

Dr. Fiore has written many journal articles in the areas of school-community relations, principal effectiveness, and school culture and has presented at numerous national and state conferences. He is the author of *Creating Connections for Better Schools: How Leaders Enhance School Culture,* and is also working on a textbook in the area of school-community relations.

Doug is married to Lisa, his wife of 12 years. They have three daughters, Meagan, 9; Amy, 6; and Katherine, 3.

Other Best-Selling Titles by Todd Whitaker

**What Great Teachers Do Differently:
Fourteen Things That Matter Most**
Todd Whitaker

**What Great Principals Do Differently:
Fifteen Things That Matter Most**
Todd Whitaker

Dealing With Difficult Teachers, 2/e
Todd Whitaker

**Dealing With Difficult Parents
(And With Parents in Difficult Situations)**
Todd Whitaker and Douglas J. Fiore

**Motivating and Inspiring Teachers:
The Educator's Guide for Building Staff Morale**
Todd Whitaker, Beth Whitaker, and Dale Lumpa

**Teaching Matters:
Motivating & Inspiring Yourself**
Todd and Beth Whitaker

**Feeling Great!
The Educator's Guide for Eating Better,
Exercising Smarter, and Feeling Your Best**
Todd Whitaker and Jason Winkle

TABLE OF CONTENTS

PREFACE

One of the most challenging and potentially unnerving tasks that educators deal with on a regular basis is interacting with parents. This may not be true of all parents, or maybe even most parents, but there is always that parent who is a special challenge. The parent who is bossy, volatile, argumentative, aggressive, or maybe the worst—apathetic—can even make us question ourselves and our abilities. As educators, we are often taken aback the first time we deal with a hostile parent. We might be uncomfortable, intimidated, or just caught off guard. However, if we do not figure out effective and appropriate ways to interact with these parents, we may become apprehensive about communicating with other parents. And eventually, this may lead to a general discomfort or fear any time we have contact with parents.

Being able to successfully interact in these situations is essential. Developing phrases to use, being able to control the dialogue, and being sensitive to trigger words to avoid are skills that are learned through experience. However, it is valuable to have specific language that is appropriate for multiple situations that allows us to accomplish our needs and hopefully even allows us to develop a more positive relationship with these parents for the future.

Another tough situation that all educators face is delivering bad news to good parents. Being able to do this effectively and in an appropriate manner is critical to developing needed support from parents. This is true whether telling parents about a discipline situation, recommending placement in a special needs program, or informing them about a child's struggles with grades. Establishing and expanding a repertoire of tools is a critical need for everyone in education.

This book will help teachers, principals, superintendents and all educators increase their skills in working with the most challenging parents you come in contact with. Additionally, educators can learn and develop specific strategies to help deliver less than positive news in an appropriate manner to all of our constituents.

We will also provide tools that can help you build credibility with all parents. This can increase the level of trust and support that is imperative in building the needed parent-school relationship, which will allow greater success for all students. Initiating positive contact with parents is essential in this process. For all educators, if we do not initiate positive contact with parents, then the only contact we may have is negative. When we get into this pattern, then we become very hesitant to inform or even interact with the adults in our students' lives. Being able to comfortably and effectively make educator-initiated contact with parents is a skill that all of us must learn and practice.

Many of the situations we face are challenging. This book will provide you with specific language, understanding, and resources that you can immediately use in interacting with every parent in your community.

1

DEALING WITH DIFFICULT PARENTS —AN OVERVIEW

There are many tasks that educators have to deal with, but there may not be any that send shivers down our spines as much as dealing with a difficult parent. Being yelled at, intimidated, threatened, or just flat-out being treated rudely are things that teachers, principals, superintendents, and everyone in education dreads having to face. And in some ways, the possibility that these things will happen, and our ability to get ourselves worked up that these things might happen, all add to the burden that we face because of difficult parents.

Additionally, having to deliver bad news to good and positive parents is also no fun. Is there some way that we can do these things more effectively? Are there specific tools that we can utilize and rely on during our most heated situations? That is the purpose of this book.

In Part I, we attempt to help you understand why parents are the way they are. Although there may be different influences and circumstances today, we also explore similarities between today's parents and those of previous generations. In Part II, we provide tools to help us refine our parental interactive skills to be more effective in communicating with all parents. You may already be using some of these, but hopefully there will be many things that we can add to our "bag of tricks."

Parts III and IV provide specific language to help educators deal effectively with our most troubling scenarios. Dialogue is provided to help us deal with our most difficult parents and work effectively with parents in the most challenging of situations. "What if the parent is right?," "The power of the apology," "Delivering bad news," and "Dealing with the 'F' word—Fair" are just a few of the situations that are described in specific detail. We also examine the power of car salesmen and learn how to be able to use their persuasive approaches to our advantage in working with the families of our students.

We also provide a section on increasing parental involvement. Traditionally we think of involved parents as those joining the PTA or volunteering to make cookies. Both of these things are important, but where children can most benefit is by parents being involved at home. We take a dual focus by centering on parental involvement at school and parental involvement with their children at home.

THE IMPORTANCE OF PARENTS

There are a couple of items that we need to clarify in this book. The first is that when we use the word *parent*, we are being very inclusive. Rather than repeatedly saying parent/ guardian or parent/grandparent or parent/adult, we rely on using the simplest approach possible—parent. We are also very sensitive to the fact that when we send home mass mailings or back-to-school night invitations, we need to be very careful with the specific way we word the salutation. We cannot flippantly use the word parent when the information is being addressed to the many different family makeups within which our students reside.

However, we also do not apologize for using that term in this book. It reminds me of using the word *teacher* when I address cooks, custodians, secretaries, bus drivers, and the like, when doing speaking engagements around the country. I always explain that if children and students see us working, then we are teachers. One way or the other, if they can observe our behavior, then we are teachers. After all, if we do not model what we teach, then we are teaching something else. Thus, the use of the word parent is for the ease of the readers, who can use the appropriate terms in their contacts with the families of their students.

WHAT'S THE DEAL WITH TODAY'S PARENTS?

The other bias that we want to share at this point is that we feel that parents are parents, and they are not really that much different than they have ever been. Parents still want what is best for their children. Now, just as 50 years ago, there will always be some parents who have no idea what is best for their children or how to provide it, but they still want it. As a matter of fact, the parents we struggle with the most now are probably the grandchildren of the parents that were most challenging 50 years ago!

If we look at any point in history, there have always been belligerent and uncooperative parents. And, realistically, those parents have always been the ones that we spend the most time dealing with, mainly because they often have the most uncooperative and belligerent children. We do believe, though, that while people are still people and parents are still parents, some environmental factors have changed. The number of single-parent homes, mothers working full time, and broken homes of all types have all been factors. We discuss these influences at length in the next two chapters. We also believe, though, that as adults we have to accept responsibility for our own behavior. If being a single parent was the cause of delinquent children, then every child from a single-parent home would be a delinquent, and we know this is not true at all. Additionally, regardless of societal influences, there is still no excuse for parents being rude or disrespectful to the professionals who are working with their children.

Yet, regardless of the cause and effect, the impact of some problem parents on the roles of educators is not in dispute, and it is something that we must work with on a regular basis. In a school where I was principal, the faculty and staff used to have a belief about the role of parents and their impact on the way their children turn out. We particularly liked to use this in the spring of the year when we were worn out and had less than ideal patience toward some of our students. When things seemed most challenging in working with a particular student or students, we would remind ourselves of this: If you have any students that you just cannot tolerate any more, you feel like your patience bucket has run out, you can barely stand the thought of them walking into your classrooms tomorrow, there is one thing that you can do. There is one simple thing you can do that will give you a whole new perspective on that child. One thing that will allow you to have a much more tolerant view of that special student. That is—meet their parents.

It is amazing, but once we meet their parents and become aware of their family situation our view of the student often changes dramatically. All of a sudden we think, "That child turned out pretty good. I thought he/she was the problem of the family, but instead it looks like he/she is probably the golden child."

This sort of became a mantra for us late in the year when we were tired and our tolerance levels were not nearly as great as they needed to be for us to be effective. We would think, "I can hardly stand thinking about Billy Edwards coming in the class anymore. I guess I'd better have a conference with his parents. After that, instead of dreading him, my empathy toward him will be greatly improved. Instead of resenting him, I'll wish I could take him home."

This view was so helpful for us. And, you need to know, we do not believe in ever generalizing in a negative manner regarding parents. As a matter of fact, we think understanding them is a critical part of our philosophy and a foundation of this book.

WE ARE DOING THE BEST WE KNOW HOW

I think it is essential to understand that 90+ percent of the parents do a pretty good job in raising their children. If we think about our schools, usually only about 5 percent of the students are a real struggle. Though all students have strengths and potential areas of growth, for the most part, parents do a pretty darn good job. But I have great faith that about 100 percent of the parents do the best they know how. We have to understand that many of their role models did not provide them the examples and structures they need to be effective parents. And, oftentimes, we compare our most troubling parents' reactions to the way our own parents would have reacted or the way the other parents in our neighborhood would have reacted. And, to be truthful, if you have a positive family structure, many parents do react in that exact same manner today. However, this book is about the most difficult and challenging parents that we work with and the most perplexing situations. We have already figured out how to deal with the easy ones; anybody can do that. What takes so much of our time, worry, and energy, is the 5 percent of the parents that we often have to deal with the most. It is important to keep a positive perspective regarding the students we work with and equally important to keep that productive focus when we think of and work with their parents. After all, they are the best parents that our students have.

Also, consistently remind yourself that we need to maintain a positive focus. One of the struggles we face is when we have back-to-school night or parent-teacher conferences and the turnout is less than we had hoped for. Regardless, we should realize that the people who do attend are our most important people, and we should not give in to the temptation to let the lack of attendance ruin our night for those who showed up. If only 10 percent of the parents are there, then make sure those 10 percent feel so special that they will not only come back in the future, but they will even spread the positive word to others.

Though we have to work with some less than pleasant individuals at times we need to focus and make sure that we do not give them to power to ruin things for the people who do show up. We provide several specific ideas for increasing the turnout at these types of events in this book, but we also need to remember that the most important people are always the ones who are there and we have to make them feel that way.

DEALING WITH YOURSELF

Dealing with difficult parents first requires that you deal with yourself. There are few absolutes in education. Generally every rule has an exception and no matter how consistent we attempt to be, there are times when we have to vary from our plan. However, there are a few things that we believe we need to be resolute about. Those things involve our own actions and approach.

The best advice I ever received was, "You do not have to prove who is in charge; everybody knows who is in charge." This is so true in schools. Think about the best teachers in your school (besides yourself, that is). How often do they have to prove "who is in charge" in their classroom? Almost never. Now, think about the least effective classroom managers in your school. How often do they try to prove who is in charge? Most likely, several times every hour! And, as a result, there are 25 students in each of their classrooms trying to prove them wrong. This same idea applies in working with challenging parents.

We never argue, yell, use sarcasm, or behave unprofessionally. The key word to focus on in that sentence is *never*. Understand that there are several reasons why we never behave in these ways. One of them is that in every situation there needs to be at least one adult, and the only person you can rely on is you. Also, one of our beliefs is you never argue with difficult people. Not only because you cannot win, which is true, but also because they have a lot more practice arguing than you do. Don't they spend a great deal of time in arguments in every aspect of their life? The people we are most likely to get in an argument with probably just spent 20 minutes arguing with the checkout clerk at the grocery store. They argue at home, are confrontational at work, and probably have a great number of interactions of this manner on a regular basis.

Another reason is a core belief of ours. We never argue with an idiot. The primary reason is because anybody watching will think that there is at least one idiot there arguing. And we do not have faith that they can tell which one of us the idiot really is.

Realize that we control how many arguments we get in. We also determine how often we yell or the frequency with which we use sarcasm. There is another, maybe more critical, reason we do not ever use these behaviors, and it is a much more important reason. A basic philosophy we have in the classroom is to never yell at students. Part of this is because it is not how we should ever treat anyone, much less the young people we work with. However, a second reason is because the students we are most tempted to yell at have probably been treated like that for much of their lives. Additionally, we need to teach them a new way to interact, not just polish their inappropriate skills.

The same thing applies to parents. If we believe they are doing the best they know how, then one of our missions should be to help them to improve. We believe we have a responsibility as educators to consistently model appropriate behaviors for everyone that we come in contact with. And, our personal view is that it needs to be 100 percent of the time. That is, we need to do it 10 days out of 10, not just 9 out of 10. If you question this, then just ask yourself two questions. "How many days out of 10 do I expect the students in my classroom and school to behave themselves?" and "How many days out of 10 do I hope that parents treat me with respect and dignity?" If this answer to these questions is 10 days out of 10, then we must ensure that we behave professionally in an equal number of days ourselves.

Though we sprinkle this book with reminders of behaving in a sincere and professional manner, please keep in mind how essential it is that we always maintain that high level of respect in our actions toward the parents that we work with. And if we do not, then we are most likely creating even more problems and turmoil for ourselves.

An example would be if we ever responded to a parent who is rude to us on the phone by hanging up on them. Though the original focus of the conversation may have been on the improper behavior of their son or daughter, once they complain about us hanging up on them, the focus often shifts to the improper behavior of us. We want to make sure that we do not add fuel to the fire by ever behaving in an inappropriate manner.

BUT I DON'T WANT
TO GO TO THE DENTIST!

Very few people race to the dentist and hope they have some significant work that needs to be done. By the same token, few among us want to deal with difficult parents. Please keep in mind that nobody wants to work with your most challenging families. This is especially true of those that are rude and offensive in the way they treat you. Please be aware that the most effective educators do not want to deal with these offensive people either. They just do.

That is why we focus an entire chapter on positive communication with parents. Making that first contact positive can go a long way in establishing the relations we want and building the credibility we hope to achieve. But the other reason we promote positive contact so much is that if we do not initiate positive contact with parents, then often the majority of the contact will be negative. Not only do the positive efforts on our part help build a bond between school and home, but they can also help build our own confidence in working with parents.

We are very excited about this project and hope that you find many tools that will be useful to you as you work with the parents and families of the young people that you have been entrusted with.

PART I

TODAY'S PARENTS

2

WHO ARE THESE GUYS? DESCRIBING TODAY'S PARENTS

Everybody is concerned with making our schools work. We all want high-quality education for our children, and we forever concern ourselves with school improvement. Because of this, the many variables that affect school improvement are important, and we all must strive to understand and manipulate them for our children's advantage. Highly important among these variables are parents. The involvement of parents in the education of their children is of unquestionable significance. Scores of studies indicate that student achievement increases as parents become more involved in their children's education (Williams et al., 1989; Epstein, 1992). Therefore, it would seem that caring, committed educators would do everything within their control to increase parent involvement in schools, thereby enriching the total school experience for the children they serve. After all, who among us would intentionally fail to do what is in the best interests of the students we serve?

However, there is something that is not significantly addressed in the studies touting the benefits of parental involvement. Simply stated, some parents are difficult to deal with. Still others live or work in very challenging situations, sometimes causing them to appear and act difficult. When we consider the proverbial full plates being juggled by the most committed educators, it is easy to understand why many of them feel that dealing with these difficult parents is an often insurmountable task. It can be, unless educators take the time to understand difficult parents and some of the difficult situations they find themselves in. Perhaps through better understanding of these difficulties, educators will feel empowered to welcome and involve parents in the education of their students.

Depending on a variety of factors (i.e., your position in a school, the demographics of your community, the most recent dealing you had with a parent), your personal, generalized description of today's parents may or may not be a positive one. All of us, at some point in our careers, are faced with difficult parents who can single-handedly destroy our faith in the institution of parenthood. In the difficult and stressful times we experience working in our schools, even the most positive among us can succumb to feelings of extreme negativity brought on by dealing with these parents. Upon reflection, though, it is hopeful that we can recognize that these difficult individuals are not necessarily representative of all parents. Beyond being hopeful, it is necessary that we remember that most parents are not intentionally difficult.

Regardless of how you, personally, describe the parents you deal with in your school setting, though, it is important for all of us to recognize that the circumstances in which parents of today find themselves may be different in some ways from the parents who raised us. Please note that there is no judgment implied in the word different. It does not mean better, and it does not mean worse. It simply means different. As such, the purpose of this chapter is not to judge parents in relation to their involvement in their children's education, but to identify ways in which they are different from those of previous generations. This knowledge will lead us to a better understanding of how to deal effectively with parents for the benefit of all children.

Outlined ahead are several of the ways in which contemporary parents and the families they lead are different from what many of us are accustomed to. The information contained is not exhaustive, nor is it descriptive of all parents. It is, however, food for thought as we learn to understand difficult parents and how to deal with them effectively. The best way to use this information is to think about it in the context of your own particular school experiences. As you read, you may find yourself conjuring up images of parents that you have worked with. This is good, for it will assist you in making the information come alive. You will understand parents best, after all, by analyzing your own experiences.

FAMILY CONFIGURATIONS

Research is replete with statistical information regarding the changes in family dynamics that our culture has experienced. Not only are there plenty of statistics to verify the changes, but our daily observations confirm them regularly. Among the factors receiving a great deal of attention in both statistics and observations is the working mother. This is one factor that makes today's parents different from those of previous generations. More and more, we see mothers of school-aged children pursuing careers or seeking full-time employment, often out of economic necessity. Consider that in 1940 fewer than 9 percent of all women with children worked outside the home (U.S. Bureau of Labor Statistics, 1987). In 1997 the U.S. Bureau of Labor Statistics reported that 76.5 percent of women with children between the ages of 6 and 13 were in the labor force (National Data Book, 1998).

This dramatic increase in the number of working mothers can be attributed to many causes, including inflation, the increased cost of child rearing, and the decreased likelihood of living the "American Dream" on a single income (Procidano and Fisher, 1992). Also contributing to this increase are the substantial rise in the United States' divorce rate and the growing percentage of women giving birth out of wedlock. As evidence, in 1995 one in three American babies was born to a single mother. This represents a dramatic shift in family configurations. In fact, while widowhood was once the primary cause of one-parent families, recent statistics indicate that 85 percent of single-parent homes result from separation or divorce, and 32 percent are the consequence of children born to mothers who've never been married (National Data Book, 1998). As we know from our observations, a very high percentage of these one-parent families are configured with the mother living with and giving primary care to the children. It is worth noting that in many cases, the term primary care is misleading. The term implies that there is somebody else giving secondary care. Yet often, many of us are finding that there is only one parent giving any care to the children. More often than not, it is the mother. In fact, of the 71,377,000 children under the age of 18 living in U.S. households in 1998, 23.3 percent, or 16,634,000, were living with their mother only (U.S. Bureau of the Census, 1999).

This apparent depreciation of fatherhood creates real problems for our schools and society. Just ask any teacher what he/she thinks the effect of fatherless homes is on students. As our experience has shown, most teachers will have strong feelings on this subject. In fact, children from fatherless homes have been found to be both less productive in school and responsible for a high percentage of criminal behavior (Blankenhorn, 1995). In addition, consider the findings of project DADS, a 1999 report from the Connecticut Department of Social Services (http://www.dss.state.ct.us/dadsdo), which reports that:

- ◆ Girls who have positive paternal involvement are three times less likely to become teenage mothers.
- ◆ Boys with involved dads are less likely to grow up unemployed, incarcerated, or uninvolved with their own children.
- ◆ Kids who team up with dads are less likely to drop out of high school.

Another example of homes that are configured differently than what many of us are used to are those in which grandparents or other relatives are the primary caregivers. The U.S. Bureau of the Census (1999) reports that 5.6 percent of U.S. children under the age of 18 are living with their grandparents. A full 36 percent of these children have no parents present in this household. These 1,417,000 children have only their grandparents to rely on for care. All educators know that these grandparents, deserving of our highest esteem for the efforts they put in to rearing the children of their children, are often more tired and in poorer health than many of them would like to be. These issues absolutely show up in our schools.

FAMILY WEALTH

In addition to the changes family configurations have undergone, the relative wealth of American households has also experienced change during the last half-century. Consider that in 1998, 14.5 million American children under the age of 18 lived in poverty (U.S. Bureau of the Census, 1999). Relating this to family configurations, 41 percent of children in families with a female head of the household and no husband present live in poverty. This is happening at a time when many are lamenting that the rich seem to be getting richer. While it is true that many families lived in poverty during other times, such as the Great Depression, the gap between the rich and the poor and the integration of the two groups within our schools and society are considered by many to be more significant today.

Another issue related to family wealth involves the high number of homeless children in this country. Children, in fact, are by most accounts among the fastest growing segments of the homeless population. Families with children constitute approximately 40 percent of people who become homeless (Shinn and Weitzman, 1990). A survey of 30 U.S. cities found that in 1998, children accounted for 25 percent of the urban homeless population (U.S. Conference of Mayors, 1998). Though we traditionally think of this as primarily an urban dilemma, these proportions are likely to be even higher in rural areas. Research indicates that families, single mothers, and children make up the largest group of people who are homeless in rural areas (Vissing, 1996). In data collected in 1998 (http://www.serve.org/nche/SEASdata.htm), it was reported that approximately 615,336 school-aged children were homeless. Additionally, 45 percent of homeless children and youth (K–12) were not attending school on a regular basis during their homelessness.

FAMILY STRESS

The wealth and configuration of a family lead to a great deal of stress in many homes. With so many parents working longer hours and being less wealthy on a relative basis than their parents reportedly were, it is no wonder that some feel that finding 15 minutes of quality time with their children is impossible. This is particularly so as schools continue to stress parent involvement during the school day, seeming to ignore the hours parents are spending at work. The result is an ever-growing percentage of parents who feel guilty that they can't be involved in their children's education. These feelings of guilt, which may be accompanied by already existing negative feelings about school that will be elaborated on later, lead many parents to become even less supportive than they would have been if our school personnel had shown some signs of understanding their plight.

There are, as we know, a multitude of reasons why families are under stress. Many of them center on issues previously discussed. In addition to the financial and structural issues, though, there is increased evidence that the adults in this country are struggling with an increase in stress-induced illnesses. This is evident when we simply look at the sharp increase in the percentage of American adults who are taking prescription drugs to deal with anxiety and other social issues.

While the previous paragraphs do not describe all of the parents that walk through the doorways of our schools, they are descriptive of an ever-growing segment of our population. School personnel need to be aware of these statistics to avoid the malady of continuing to filter our images of the world through the lenses of our own experiences. We can no longer afford to judge parents solely on the basis of how involved they appear to be in their children's education. Likewise, we cannot blindly accept the lack of involvement because we know that parents play a critical role in the education of their children. Moreover, we cannot delight in the absence of our more difficult parents. Though this is often a natural reaction, as working with these difficult parents can be very annoying and time-consuming, the absence of even our difficult parents means that we lose some valuable resource help. This is simply not fair to our students. What is needed is an understanding of today's parents, a realization that many of them do not feel that they possess the resources to be actively involved in their children's education, a commitment to enable their involvement, and the strategies available for dealing with them when they seem to be so difficult.

TYPICAL BEHAVIORS OF SOME OF OUR PARENTS

Thinking back to some of the difficult situations that we have been involved in with parents is not often a pleasant form of relaxation. Often the experience is reminiscent of "nails on a chalkboard." Nevertheless, by reminding ourselves of some of these situations we can begin to see patterns that can be helpful when we find ourselves in similar situations in the future. Our goal, in recognition of the many benefits associated with schools having positive relationships with parents, ought to be to learn from these situations. By understanding how to effectively deal with parents, particularly those living through many of the difficulties previously described, we can turn negative situations into very positive ones.

We can certainly come up with many examples of difficult parents and difficult situations from our own experiences as teachers and administrators. In fact, the odds are very good that you will be able to relate some of your own experiences with those that follow:

One example is the parent who marches into the principal's office complaining that his/her child's teacher does not recognize the child's innate abilities. Regardless of the grade levels served by your school, it can be said with relative certainty that all of you can relate to this experience. In this particular instance, let's say that we are speaking of a kindergarten student. The parent, and it can be either mom or dad, is convinced that the child is gifted. The issue that the parent finds so upsetting is that the teacher has stated that the child does not know his/her address. The parent, obviously enraged by this, comes to see the principal insisting that something be done about this incompetent teacher. In fact, this parent insists, this particular child has been reciting his/her home address for a full eight months!

Consider a second example. Again, though virtually any grade level could be substituted into the following situation, let's say that we are dealing with a student in the eleventh grade. This particular student has gotten into a fight during a passing period between classes. In this fight, he/she threw several punches, caused injury to another student, spoke disrespectfully to a teacher, and brought chaos to an otherwise normal part of the school day. As punishment for this fight, the principal has issued a one-day suspension from school activities. The parent, again either mom or dad will do, comes in to school to see the principal. The only apparent purpose for this meeting is to find out what punishment the other student who was involved in the altercation received. Despite the principal's best efforts to keep the conversation focused on the appropriate issues, the parent does not relent and continues to demand an explanation of the other child's punishment.

Though not issues that are going to single-handedly drive too many administrators into early retirement, these examples typify some of the time-consuming parent issues that educators are increasingly dealing with. The issues are not confining themselves to the principal's office either, as they may have years ago. Instead, teachers, custodians, bus drivers, and other school employees are facing them as well. Without knowledge of some techniques for dealing with these situations, professional work in public schools begins to seem less and less appealing to some. Without some sense of why parents behave like this, any effort at understanding how to resolve these issues seems fruitless. However, as many of us realize, there are reasons why some parents behave similarly to those in the previous examples. Several of these reasons will be explored in subsequent chapters. Remember, parents, in many ways, are different than any of us think they ought to be. Given their circumstances, however, they are not necessarily wrong. But since they are different, dealing with them, in many cases, requires understandings and strategies that are different than what we might otherwise expect. As this book will clearly illustrate, there are specific behaviors, strategies, and techniques that will make it so much easier to deal with seemingly difficult parents and with the difficult situations they find themselves in. The first step is to understand parents. It is only after we make an honest effort in this regard that we can really hope to employ practices to effectively deal with them.

Remember, parental involvement is a key in many of our best schools. It is, many believe, a significant variable in student success. School leaders—and for our purposes all educators are considered school leaders—must recognize and then manipulate this important variable. As leaders for all children, we owe it to them to do all that we can to understand and subsequently embrace our most difficult parents. Their involvement, too, will be a key in improving our schools.

As you read the remainder of this book, you will discover examples that sound much like some of those that you have lived through in your own school. You will read practical solutions that are not difficult to emulate. Finally, you will come to understand the value of dealing effectively with difficult parents in a way that will make your job as educator that much more appealing.

3

What's Wrong with These Parents Anyway?

A description of today's parents and the situations they face assists us in understanding what American family life is like and how different it is than family life may have been when we were growing up. This is important only to the extent that it affirms the differences educators have been suspecting. It does little, however, in terms of explaining just what's wrong with these parents anyway. It fails, in many ways, to explain why parents behave as they do. Examining the information available to contemporary parents and what this information says about our educational systems is of real value in our understanding why some parents view our schools with negative feelings. In addition, an understanding of the experiences that today's parents had when they were schoolchildren sheds light on the seemingly dark reactions some of them may have toward our schools.

PERCEPTION IS REALITY

Take a walk down the aisles of your favorite bookstore and you'll find many titles designed to either assist parents in holding their children's schools accountable or inform them of the functions, structures, and/or problems in our schools. Recent titles that have been purchased by many of our schools' parents include *Beyond the Classroom: Why School Reform Has Failed and What Parents Need to Do* (Steinberg, 1997), *Angry Parents, Failing Schools: What's Wrong with the Public Schools & What You Can Do About It* (McEwan, 1998a), *Bad Teachers: The Essential Guide for Concerned Parents* (Strickland, 1998), *Waiting For a Miracle: Why Schools Can't Solve Our Problems—And How We Can* (Comer,

1998), *Parental Involvement and the Political Principle: Why the Existing Governance Structure of Schools Should Be Abolished* (Sarason, 1995). A quick glance at these titles would lead one to believe that parents have at their disposal a plethora of information condemning our schools.

In fairness to the above-mentioned authors, the condemnation of our schools was probably not their goal while writing these books. In fact, in defense of some of them, we can say with certainty that it was not their goal. However, a mere reading of these book titles clearly suggests that there is something wrong with the schools our children are attending. Furthermore, there is an implication that parents must do something about it. With this in mind, what kind of message are parents receiving when they look at these titles on bookstore shelves? Are they receiving a message touting the quality of our work and applauding our efforts? Obviously not. It is true that you cannot judge a book by its cover. You can, however, have feelings invoked by the wording of titles and the intonations they suggest. This is one of the reasons journalists give for the headlines we find in our daily newspapers. Because a vast majority of the population does not read a newspaper from cover to cover, journalists must use article titles to "grab" readers and make them want to read.

If you have had the uncomfortable experience of having a parent share one of these books with you, you will understand this even better. Now, consider this. If a parent, already dissatisfied with the way in which they perceive your school to be dealing with their child, encounters books like those mentioned above, then one can bet that their dissatisfaction will be heightened. Of greater concern, though, is the reaction of parents who do not already harbor these feelings of dissatisfaction. What might their response to the suggestions of these titles be? Is it conceivable that without ever reading one word of the text, they might begin to question whether or not they have correctly been assessing their child's school? Might they, in fact, become less supportive and more suspicious, without any real basis for these attitudinal changes? Along the continuum of school supporters, with our most supportive parents on one end and our most difficult ones on the other, are there parents at any point who would have their opinions of our schools improved by glancing at these book titles? Such a notion appears preposterous.

Again, the content of some of these books may, in fact, lead to improved feelings of support from parents. If only the tiles are read, however, then such a result is highly unlikely. What we unfortunately wind up with instead is a growing segment of the population with distorted perceptions who claim that our schools are failing. We now face an increased struggle to correct these misperceptions. Remember, to many people, perception is reality. In our work as school principals, a major thrust of our efforts was always to positively alter people's perceptions of our schools. It is very important to remember though that there are many people working against these efforts.

FAMILY FOCUS: CHILDREN OR ADULTS?

In addition to the print and mass media treatment schools receive in contemporary society, we must look again at the very structure and functionality of today's families. One way to assess these issues is to examine the subtle changes society has seen in parenting practices. According to some social psychologists, families can be classified as being either child centered or adult centered. In reality, most families certainly exhibit behavior from both classifications. Child-centered families, often represented by the middle class, are recognized as those families that focus their resources on the needs of their children. By contrast, adult-centered families, typically thought of as lower class or underclass families, tend to use available resources to satisfy the needs of adults, not children. It is important to note that economic classifications of families do not necessarily dictate whether they are child center or adult centered. The tendencies are as we have mentioned, however.

Rather than judging all adult-centered behavior, we need to understand that in some cases an adult-centered attitude grows out of the difficulty in coping with the demands of daily life. These adult-centered, or self-centered, parents spend much of their time worrying about basic needs, such as food and shelter. Consequently, children and the things they need are often pushed to the rear. In addition to the apparent dysfunction this creates, children in adult-centered families do not have as much attention paid to their academic needs as do children in child-centered families. The result is less parent involvement at school, lower expectations, and poorer achievement. When families have the resources and/or the desires to be child centered, then the needs of the children become a focal point in family life.

In your own school experiences, you have probably seen these descriptions played out numerous times. Depending on the population served by your school, most readers have probably struggled with adult-centered families. As a result, many readers have probably complained from time to time that parents do not seem to care about their children. We need to understand that for some, but not all, of these families there simply is no alternative.

Both authors can recall times when our hearts have been broken upon the realization that some of our students were not receiving adequate attention at home. Such thoughts as "If I could just take this child home with me..." or "Why don't these parents care?" crossed our minds as they have crossed the minds of many of you. Difficult though it may be, we all need to realize that the apparent lack of care shown in adult-centered families is often masking a deeper problem. For many of these families, though clearly not all of them, there really is not any choice.

It is also worth noting here that child-centered behavior can be taken to extremes that are equally as damaging as adult-centered behaviors are when they are taken to extremes. Recalling some of our own experiences, we can certainly recall parents who overindulged their children and became, in some cases, our most difficult parents to work with. The overindulgence experienced by their children created an unrealistic sense of self, which sometimes led to the child getting into serious trouble at school. The parents, expert at overindulging the child, always defended the child's actions, even when they were clearly wrong. Have you ever had experiences like that? These, too, can be difficult to deal with.

NEGATIVE SCHOOL EXPERIENCES

As educators, we must be mindful of the fact that many of our parents did not have favorable experiences when they were schoolchildren. In fact, attending school during an era that placed less emphasis on affective education than contemporary schools do, many of these parents do not view schools as places that concern themselves with the feelings and attitudes of the students. Also, in light of the many changes that have taken place in regard to the education of children with special needs, many parents still remember back to the days when we were not quite so sensitive about different abilities. The only opinions that really mattered in determining a student's educational goals were those of school personnel. These parents, therefore, are not used to having their opinions count in educational settings. Despite the cries from our schools asking for parent involvement, many parents are skeptical about our sincerity. They suspect that their presence makes us uncomfortable, and that we would be just as happy if they stayed home and let us do our jobs. The cause of these negative school experiences is irrelevant. It makes little difference whether a parent views school negatively because of their own lack of effort to succeed or because of their perception that school failed them. The importance lies in the fact that the mere mention of the word "school" conjures up negative images for some of our parents.

Many parents who do view schools favorably and who do believe our invitations for involvement are sincere become disenchanted by the ritualized systems that we have created for their involvement. Although many schools, as will be outlined in subsequent chapters, do provide new and different ways for parents to be involved, many are still mired in the traditional rituals we disguise as parent involvement opportunities. Consider, for example, the traditional open-house program in which parents are urged to come to school to listen to teachers explain rules and expectations for the school year.

Usually, there is little opportunity for interaction between parent and teacher. This lack of interaction can cause an unintended gap to be created between teacher and parent, thereby reducing the chance that the parent will choose to be involved in future school activities. As Sara Lawrence Lightfoot (1978) explains:

> Schools organize public, ritualistic occasions that do not allow for real contact, negotiation, or criticism between parents and teachers. Rather, they are institutionalized ways of establishing boundaries between insiders (teachers) and interlopers (parents) under the guise of polite conversation and mature cooperation. Parent-Teacher Association meetings and open house rituals at the beginning of the school year are contrived occasions that symbolically affirm the idealized parent-school relationship but rarely provide the chance for authentic interaction. (pp. 27–28)

Schools, therefore, need to examine the procedures that they have in place for encouraging parental involvement. School leaders need to structure activities, which make it easier and more natural for positive interaction between parent and teacher to take place. Teachers need to be supportive of these efforts, ever mindful of the benefits students will experience as a result.

While there are plenty of difficult parents who appear not to care about their children's education, it is important to remember that many parents from all kinds of backgrounds do care about the education their children receive at school. Additionally, they do support the efforts of the school and recognize the significance of their role in the educational process. However, school personnel must realize that the diverse background of some of our parents creates a necessity for us to educate them about the importance of their involvement. We speak openly in many of our schools about the need to be "multicultural." Yet, as we have observed, in many schools the dominant culture still rules supremely. Caring school principals and teachers must recognize that involvement and specific roles and responsibilities mean different things in different cultures. Consider the perception of many Asian immigrant parents. Due to cultural differences, many of these parents view communication with teachers as "checking up on them" and as an expression of disrespect (Yao, 1988). As a result, what appears to be apathy is more likely, in these cases, to be a sign of respect. Other cultures hold similar views. Unless they receive sincere, personal invitations to become involved, many American parents will continue to stay away; not out of disdain, but out of respect. We must recognize this.

ANGRY PARENTS

As most veterans of education can attest to, there are some parents who appear to be "just plain angry." They may be angry for a variety of reasons, including some of those already mentioned in this book. As educators, we are trained to search for answers to these and similar problems. We do this to a fault at times. Analyzing angry parents may be a perfect example. Rather than trying to understand precisely what it is that makes some parents angry with us, we must look for ways to deal with their anger for the benefit of our students. If our goal in dealing with an angry parent is to understand why they are angry and then to convince them not to be angry, we are often doomed to failure. Let's instead focus on better ways to deal with the anger itself. As Stephen Covey says in describing an important habit of interpersonal effectiveness, "Seek first to understand, then to be understood" (Covey, 1990, p. 255). In doing so, we will find ourselves diffusing more situations and ensuring that our focus in all conversations with parents is what's best for their children.

In future chapters, we will discuss some specific techniques for dealing with angry parents. For now, consider this tale:

> On a path that went by a village in Bengal, there lived a cobra who used to bite people on their way to worship at the temple there. As the incidents increased, everyone became fearful, and many refused to go to the temple. The Swami who was the

master at the temple was aware of the problem and took it upon himself to put an end to it. Taking himself to where the snake dwelt, he used a mantra to call the snake to him and bring it into submission. The Swami then said to the snake that it was wrong to bite the people who walked along the path to worship and made him promise sincerely that he would never do it again. Soon it happened that the snake was seen by a passerby upon the path, and it made no move to bite him. Then it became known that the snake had somehow been made passive and people grew unafraid. It was not long before the village boys were dragging the poor snake along behind them as they ran laughing here and there. When the temple Swami passed that way again, he called the snake to see if he had kept his promise. The snake humbly and miserably approached the Swami, who exclaimed, "You are bleeding. Tell me how this has come to be." The snake was near tears and blurted out that he had been abused ever since he was caused to make his promise to the Swami. "I told you not to bite," said the Swami, "but I did not tell you not to hiss."

In examining the many messages of this story, we can come to an understanding of anger and the responses it requires. First of all, let's examine the emotional state of the cobra. In completely suppressing his anger, he wound up getting taken advantage of and walked all over. This is why many parents are unable and unwilling to completely suppress their own anger. It is also why we, as educators, don't always completely suppress our own angry feelings. Human nature and what we have all learned about sound negotiation strategy has left us fearful of being taken advantage of. However, as your own experience has surely demonstrated, becoming angry at an angry parent rarely does any good.

Next, consider the Swami's final statement to the cobra. When he says, "I told you not to bite, but I did not tell you not to hiss," he is explaining that there are appropriate ways to show our emotions. Parents who lash out at us in verbal abuse are obviously "biting." This behavior is inappropriate and need not be tolerated. In fact, if a parent does engage in inappropriate, abusive behavior, then we have a responsibility to make it clear that such behavior is unacceptable. On the other hand, those who question us and show disapproval toward some of our decisions are merely "hissing." We must know the difference. In knowing the difference, we must also take care to be less sensitive when we are being hissed at. We also must assist those who are biting to learn to hiss instead. Finally, we must take care to never bite back.

It is perfectly normal for us to wish that parents would not get angry with us. It is safe to assume that nobody enjoys having people angry with him or her. It is also normal for us to yearn for the day, real or imagined, when parents did not ever show us angry feelings. In accepting reality, though, we understand that some parents are angry. This anger, whether we like it or not, will get expressed. We need to act as the Swami, insisting that parents hiss instead of bite, and acknowledging that anger does need to be expressed sometimes. The importance is in both the appropriateness of the expression and in our method for dealing with it. In Part II, we address important considerations for communicating effectively with parents. Parts III and IV provide a great deal of practical advice for dealing with angry or difficult parents.

PART II

COMMUNICATING WITH PARENTS

4

BUILDING CREDIBILITY— EVERYONE WANTS TO ASSOCIATE WITH A WINNER

It is amazing what an incredible thing trust is. If we trust someone, he or she can tell us almost anything and we will believe him/her. By the same token, if we don't trust someone, he or she can tell us almost anything and there is not much chance we will believe him/her. The same thing is true regarding our relationship with the parents of the students in our classes. If we can establish trust with them, they will allow us great discretion in decisions that we make. However, if they do not trust us, then they inspect everything we do with a high-powered microscope. Knowing this, how can we develop that bond with parents so that at the very least we can get the benefit of the doubt? Is there a way to nurture that relationship to the degree that we can develop a culture and spirit of mutual regard which will allow us a much wider swath of trust? It can happen in all schools with all educators, but it is definitely something that we have to work at.

IF THEY DON'T HEAR GOOD NEWS FROM YOU

One of the first challenges that schools face is developing a positive image. Unfortunately, oftentimes the newspapers, radio talk shows, and many political officials will take potshots at schools and teachers. Part of this is because they hear other people do it. On a sports radio call-in show one time, a 9- or 10-year-old boy called in criticizing a former St. Louis Cardinal catcher named Ted Simmons. The boy lamented, "Simmons is lazy. He can't hit, he can't run, he can't throw, and he was a bad influence on the team! In addition, he is way overpaid and a bad role model in the clubhouse."

The wise talk show host said, "It sounds like somebody has been listening around the supper table." Well, we think it sounds like a lot of people have been listening around the water cooler. We all see ourselves as educational experts simply because we all went to school. How does the old quote go? *If we took every critic of education and laid them end-to-end...they would be a lot more comfortable.*

We also know that people in general view their local schools in a much more favorable light than they do schools on a national basis. Additionally, parents view the schools their children attend more positively than do community members without children in school. With this in mind, what can we do to build credibility and trust with all of our constituents?

EVERYONE WANTS TO ASSOCIATE WITH A WINNER

Understand that everyone wants to associate with a winner. If you ever question it, just look at your local college basketball team. The team that struggles the most needs more fan support than ever, but seldom does this occur. Instead, the most successful teams tend to consistently pack the house. It is interesting, but there aren't nearly as many Chicago Bulls fans since Michael Jordan retired than there were when he was still playing and the Bulls were still winning!

With this in mind, how can we best develop the belief that our school is a winner? Let's start with the basic notion of open-house or back-to-school night. What does your school do to promote the event? Does your student council have an evening in which they attempt to call every single family and personally invite them to back to school night? Regardless of the size of the school, you could develop a short script for the students to read in which they encourage every family to attend back-to-school night. Set a goal so that every household receives one phone call inviting them to open-house night. If the students receive an answering machine when they call, then they leave a message. If no one answers, then they move to the next one on the list.

Moving from a schoolwide basis to an individual teacher basis, you could personally call the parents of every student you have and invite them to attend. If you are in a departmental setting with vast numbers of students, then perhaps you could get a few parent volunteers or students to assist. We realize this is a lot of work, but it is amazing the rewards it will reap.

In addition, the individual classrooms could hold a contest to see which homerooms have the largest percentage of students represented. In other words, if a homeroom has 30 students and 18 of the students have at least one person attend back-to-school night, they would have a 60 percent representation. Regardless of whether students had one, two, or five people from their family come, it would still count as one. Then, the principal or parent volunteers could serve donuts to the winning homeroom the next day. If you could not get the schoolwide organization going, then there could be a contest among a grade level, team, or department. Obviously what we do when we get them there is the next step.

Understand that regardless of whether we have 20 or 1000 people come to our open house we need to make sure that the ones that do attend feel special. *Do not* focus on the people who are not there. Instead, make sure that the ones who did come have a very positive feeling about their attendance. Make sure that you warmly greet everyone that you see. If the parents can have an initial positive impression of you, that can help temper future issues that may arise. Even more important, if they develop a negative impression that may be difficult, if not impossible, to overcome. Having open house as early as possible in the school year or even right before school starts may be the best timing. No one has "been in trouble yet," and we are all still undefeated. Making a positive impression before we would have to deliver bad news is essential in building trust.

Chapter 5 provides some specific ideas on ways to make those positive contacts. One thing to keep in mind is that if we suspect that at some point we might have to deliver bad news to a parent we might want to make it a special point to deliver good news quickly so that the positive interaction can be our first contact and impression with them.

Here is another idea at open house that we have found to be simple and yet very effective. When one of us was a principal, in front of the entire auditorium full of families, I would tell parents to call me anytime—at school or at home. I would then tell them my home phone number is in the book and if they want to write it down it is 555-8493. It was amazing the stunned looks that I would get on the parents' faces when I did this. If you were a parent in the auditorium how would that make you feel?

The first time I did this at open house night, a faculty member asked how I could possibly encourage people to call me at home like that. I replied, "The few irrational parents we have can always find your home number, and they will call you at home regardless. However, this approach makes everyone in that auditorium feel that someone cares about them and their child." Years later parents would tell me that they always remembered that. The other benefit, of course, was that numerous teachers in the school would see it and then follow this role-modeled behavior. Then in many classrooms throughout the school I would observe that teachers would write their home phone numbers on the board in their classrooms.

I can imagine that you are thinking to yourself that you already receive too many phone calls at home. Relax, you will not receive more calls at night. As a matter of fact, I think I received less. I had numerous parents tell me, "I was going to call you at home. I know you said we could, but I figured you get so many calls that I decided that I did not want to ever bother you at night." They felt better about me, and I actually had more of a personal life. This exact approach is just as appropriate and effective in each individual classroom setting. Every teacher can build and grow a higher level of trust with the parents of their students by using this approach.

LET ME INTRODUCE MYSELF

Another technique that we can do in our classrooms is to call every students' household before school starts and introduce ourselves to them and/or their parents. You can say something as basic as, "Hi. I'm Caroline Jones and I will be DeJuan's fourth grade teacher this year. I am really looking forward to having him in class and I just wanted to call and introduce myself." You could also ask if they have any questions or tell a little bit about your personal background. If the open-house night is coming up, you could combine this call with an invitation to attend.

A similar activity would be to have a "Welcome back to school!" picnic for the students and parents. You could send postcards announcing the date, time, and place and even ask people to bring a dish to share. Starting with positive contact can help establish a very productive relationship with parents.

TOUCHING BASE

Not only is the idea of touching base a good idea at the start of the year, it is equally effective at any time during the year. Calling one or two families a week can allow us to spread out the work and still touch base. Just asking a parent in October how things are going so far can be of great benefit throughout the year and help solidify the trust that we have established.

Again, when I was a principal, one of my favorite things to do was to touch base with a parent who had expressed concern over a situation in the school a week or two later to ask how things were going. To be honest, I especially liked to do this when I knew things were going better. I might ask the student how everything was going in regard to the previous troubling situation. After he or she shared that things were going great, I would then call his/her parents and ask for their perspective. Though I might have already known what the answer would be, the real benefit was to show care and concern toward their child. This can have a long-lasting and positive impact. And, since things really were going well, it was a chance to have a positive contact with the parents. This would be doubly important if I felt this was going to be a challenging parent to work with or if they happened to be married to a school board member!

REACHING OUT
TO THE COMMUNITY

Making a positive impression throughout the community is also an important step. Consistently contact local television and radio stations as well as print media outlets with every piece of good news that you can think of. And if they ignore you? Then just keep after them. Find out if you have any parents with media contacts or if your business partner may have access. This is something that can be done on an individual-teacher or whole-school basis.

Another way to reach out and potentially get positive recognition is by doing community service projects. Your class could adopt a local nursing home or do a service project by cleaning up a local park. An athletic team you coach could go to a retirement center and sing Christmas Carols to the group. I used to do this with my varsity boys basketball team, and it was amazing how beneficial this was for the team as well as positive for the community. When you do special projects like this, make sure that you inform the media and put it in your school classroom newsletter. Coupling the positive experiences with beneficial publicity is an important facet of building up credibility.

MY NEWS IS GOOD NEWS

Many schools have regular parent newsletters. In addition, many classroom teachers, middle school teams, or high school departments have monthly, weekly, or even daily newsletters that are routinely shared with parents and families. These tools are an important way to make sure that we represent ourselves and our role in the most positive light possible.

The National Association of Elementary School Principals (1993) produced a checklist of newsletter DOs and DON'Ts.

This is a nice foundation for the documents that we develop and share with the families of our students.

NEWSLETTER DOs AND DON'Ts

Do: Be Personal. Write as if you are on a home visit— using "we" and "ours." Be chatty but avoid too many capital letters and exclamation points!!!!!

Do: Be Brief. If it takes more than 10 minutes to read, it's too long.

Do: Be Professional. Keep the focus on what children are learning and how parents can reinforce it.

Do: Include Names. People love to read their and their child's name in print.

Do: Include a Calendar. At least 6 weeks in advance for special events.

Do: Ask For Feedback. Have a short survey.

Don't: Use Jargon.

Don't: Preach. Discuss major problems in another format.

Don't: Assume. Your readers may not be familiar with a subject. Continuously redefine items.

Don't: Limit Distribution. The more the merrier. School board, superintendent, neighborhood businesses, leave copies out around the school.

FOCUS ON THE PEOPLE
WHO ARE DOING THINGS RIGHT!

One thing that is so critical in a newsletter, memo, or any other correspondence that goes out to the masses is to make sure that we constantly focus on the people who are doing things right, not those who are doing things wrong.

We once saw a newsletter that lectured parents to always pick up their kids promptly after a field trip and sternly warned that if they did not, the students would be placed in an after-school care program, for which the parents would be charged $2.00 an hour. One of the most interesting aspects of this newsletter was that it came out at the end of May, the last week of school. Understand what happens with this approach. People are already aware that they should pick up their children promptly; it is just that some forgot or maybe even don't care. Realize that those people either will not read the newsletter, cannot read the newsletter, or do not care even if they do read the newsletter. Instead, the 95+ percent of parents who are responsible are left with a negative taste in their mouths because of the tone of the piece. Additionally, reminding people at the end of the school year what they had *better* do the next year is fruitless at best. The other irony was that some parents might even read it and say, "Oh, I didn't know they had after-school care as a possibility when my child gets back from a field trip. That is great. Now I do not have to be in a hurry to get them and that $2.00-an-hour rate is cheaper than what I pay the sitter."

Instead, work on preventative maintenance by sending home friendly reminders with parents whenever they have field trips. We realize that will not always work, but at least we are not insulting all of the positive and responsible parents in our school.

5

POSITIVE COMMUNICATION WITH PARENTS— AN OUNCE OF PREVENTION

One challenge that all educators face is building credibility with parents. We often hear from teachers and administrators that parents do not respect educators like they did in the "good old days." Stories are shared that when "we" were growing up, if the school called and said you got a 5-swat paddling at school, then you would get a 10-swat whipping when you got home. Sometimes teachers-lounge talk laments that their word used to be bond and now there is little or no support at all from the home. Teachers sometimes say that they feel like the Rodney Dangerfield of professions in that they "don't get no respect."

However, even if it is true that educators no longer automatically have respect from all the parents, there is a way to build and nurture credibility even with the most challenging of families.

POSITIVE PHONE CALLS

When I first became an assistant principal in charge of discipline and supervision at a junior high school, I remember looking at my job description wondering what the good things about my job were. I looked at the first page of the description and then turned it over and read the second page. After reading the entire document, I sat back and still wondered what the good things about my job would be.

I realized if I just waited for things to happen, I was only going to deal with students when they were in trouble, teachers when they had a problem, and especially with parents when they were upset. Well, I knew this was no way to function or enjoy my job. I quickly realized I could get into classrooms regularly and be visible throughout the school. This would allow me to have some positive interaction with students and teachers and assist me in beginning to establish some credibility with them during neutral or positive times.

However, this still did not allow me to have some positive interaction with parents. I felt that to do so was essential, basically because I would have to have a great deal of less positive contact when I called them with punishments, detentions, suspensions, and the like, as assistant principal responsible for discipline of 700+ eighth graders. Also, I was well aware that if the students went home and said positive things about me, that would also help the parents think of me in a more positive light.

When I was an assistant principal, I realized that it was up to me whether I was going to enjoy my job or not. If I just waited around for things to happen, they surely would. Unfortunately, most of the things that come the way of an assistant principal responsible for discipline of 750 eighth graders, tend to be negative. I then determined that it is *my* responsibility to meld my job so that it would be enjoyable to come to work each day. In order to try to maintain a little balance in my job, I started a *positive referral* program.

Most schools have discipline referrals, where teachers "write up" kids for misbehavior and then send them to the office with the referral form. Assistant principals often deal with the majority of these situations. However, I felt that it was at least as important to have a positive referral program. This was a form that was similar in format, only we put it on bright red paper. Teachers would "write up" students for doing positive things. It could be that Tim got a B+ on a math quiz, they enjoy seeing Megan's smiling face every day, or Juan helped a student who was on crutches move around the school for a week. As long as it was something authentic, it was appropriate to write up a positive referral and put it in my mailbox.

When I pulled the positive referral out of my mailbox, I would send for the student. Initially, students were nervous, frightened, or defensive when they were summoned to the office. Often students would walk in and immediately tell the secretary, "It wasn't me!" When I called the student into my office, I would first congratulate them and tell them how proud I was of their accomplishment. I would share with them which teacher referred them and why they did so. I would thank them for their contribution to making our school a better place.

This, in and of itself may have been enough and it definitely helped establish credibility and positive relations with students. However, I took it one step further. I would pick up the phone and call the child's parent. And, if they had two parents, I would call the one that worked. And, if both parents worked, I would call the one that worked in the busiest office or on the most crowded factory assembly line. Let's think for a moment what those phone calls were like. Here is an example involving calling Kenny Johnson's mother at work for a positive referral.

"Hi. Mrs. Johnson, this is Bill Smith, assistant principal at Meadow Grove Middle School."

As you can imagine, this conversation was usually interrupted at this point by the parent with a loud moan, "Oh, no!"

I would then continue with the conversation; "Mrs. Johnson, I am sorry to bother you at work, but I just thought you might want to know that Kenny's teacher, Mrs. Smith, is running around up here at school, bragging on your son. She sent me a positive referral saying that Kenny did an excellent job working with his group leading a science experiment yesterday. I called Kenny down to the office to congratulate him and I wanted to call and share the good news with you."

The conversation then would typically continue in a very positive manner and I would let the parent know that the student was in the office with me and that he or she was welcome to talk with them.

A lot of principals have positive referrals and other programs in their schools. This is wonderful. However, the added twist of calling the parents at work led to several significant and positive contributions for me. Interestingly, the most frequent comment I received from parents was, "A school has never called with anything good before." This was consistently the theme when I called hundreds and hundreds of parents. It did not matter if I was contacting the parent of a student who was frequently in trouble or the future valedictorian. Parents had never had unsolicited, positive contact from anyone at school.

Though I thought this was very sad, it did help me realize a couple of things. First, I finally understood why people believe the criticism of schools and teachers they read in the newspapers. I now was also able to comprehend why people buy into the nonsense that they hear on radio call-in shows criticizing educators and schools in America . It is because if they do not hear good news from us, the public may never hear *good* news about schools and teachers. Thus, it is critically important that we consistently initiate positive contact with parents.

At this point you may be asking yourself a couple of things. "Why did you call parents specifically at work?" and "This is all fine and dandy, but what does it have to do with building credibility with parents?" Well, let me take a stab at both of those questions.

I called the parents at work for a very selfish reason. It relates to the publicity issue. When I called Mrs. Johnson and her initial reaction was a loud "Oh, no!", do you have any guess what the first thing she did was in that crowded office when she hung up the phone? She told everybody in the office! And, I do not know about you, but I do not mind people saying good things about me and my school in public. I also know there was an office full of other parents who were thinking to themselves that their child's school never has called with good news. Anything that builds the reputation of you and your school does nothing but help parents see you in a more positive light. And your relationship with the parents is also greatly enhanced.

Additionally, there were a couple of other selfish benefits involved in this whole process for me. If I had previously initiated positive contact with a parent, it is amazing how that impacted future calls, especially if I had to call the parent at some future point with less than good news. Let's pretend I had to call Mrs. Johnson several weeks later over a discipline matter.

"Hi. Mrs. Johnson, this is Bill Smith, assistant principal at Meadow Grove Middle School."

And Mrs. Johnson would reply, "Hi. How are you today?"

At first, I was so shocked by Mrs. Johnson's friendly response that I would assume she had not understood me! But, eventually I would continue:

"Mrs. Johnson, I am sorry to bother you at work, but today Kenny was involved in an incident where he . . . (was fighting, sent to the office, etc.) and as a result he will be receiving... (detention, suspension, etc.)."

Then, Mrs. Johnson would respond by using the "F" word on me. She would say, "That's okay. I know you're *fair*. You call me with good news and you call me with bad news. You can call me anytime you want."

What I quickly learned was that making positive referrals may have seemed like additional work, but it really made my job easier. I had built relationships with parents that had significant positive impacts down the line. My job just became more tolerable. However, the real benefit from making positive phone calls was even more selfish. They also made me feel better about my job and more confident in interacting with parents.

Interestingly, the reaction to this approach was so positive that the local newspaper and television stations gave the positive referral program wonderful publicity. This helped my school and me to be regularly put into a very positive light in the community and with parents.

After two years of doing this as assistant principal, I became principal, and the entire faculty decided to participate by making one positive phone call a week. When we first talked about this at a staff meeting, we realized that very few of us had ever made positive contact with parents. We then came to the conclusion that because of this omission, the only contact we ever had with parents was negative. We also decided that, for the most part, we were afraid of parents. Since such a large percentage of the time when parents contact us it is for something less than positive, we gradually became hesitant or even reluctant to interact with and especially initiate contact with students' parents and families.

We also realized that, believe it or not, we did not really know how to praise or what we should say when we do call parents with good news. Let's first take a look at the components of praise.

FIVE THINGS THAT
HELP PRAISE WORK

One of the challenges that all educators face is learning how to praise. That may seem silly, but often teachers have spent their whole careers looking for what is wrong, pointing out errors, and focusing on mistakes. This is a part of being an educator. However, an educational *leader* looks for opportunities to find people doing things right. One of the difficulties for many educators is truly understanding praise and being able to apply it on a daily basis.

Ben Bissell (1992) has described five things that help praise work. He feels that these are important elements in order for praise attempts to have the most positive effect possible. The five things Dr. Bissell indicates are characteristics of effective praise are authentic, specific, immediate, clean, and private. Let us apply these general characteristics to the specifics of building credibility with parents.

Authentic means that we are praising people for something genuine, recognizing them for something that is true. This is an important facet because the recognition of something authentic can never grow weary. Sometimes people state that they do not praise more because they feel that it will lose its credibility or become less believable if it happens too much. The way to prevent this is to make sure that it is always authentic. No one ever feels that they are praised too much for something genuine. Authentic does not mean that it is earth-shattering or a magnificent accomplishment. Instead, the only requirement is that it be true. As educators, we have many opportunities to catch students doing things right. Remembering them, writing them down, and then making it a point to share them with the parents of your students is essential in developing positive relations.

The second characteristic of effective praise is *specific*. The behavior we acknowledge often becomes the behavior that will be continued. If we can recognize students' positive efforts with specific recognition, then we can help them see specific areas of value. For example, you might acknowledge that a student gave forth an excellent effort in class or assisted another student who was on crutches. Specific praise also allows you to reinforce someone in an authentic manner. If you use specific praise, you can recognize everyone in your classroom or even in your school. Even students that are struggling can still be praised. You do not have to be dishonest and say they are the smartest student in class, or that they got the highest grade on a test, if they did not. Instead, you can identify those areas that did have merit and acknowledge them through praise to their parents.

The third item is *immediate*. This means recognizing positive efforts and contributions in a timely manner. This is especially true when we think of our more challenging students. We realized that it was essential to have positive contact with parents *before* we might need to have to make a negative phone call. Thus, when we had potentially challenging students in our classrooms, we made positive phone calls to their parents as soon as there were any behaviors we could reinforce. It was amazing, but we realized that this approach saved us much consternation and grief in dealing with this parent at a later date under less positive circumstances.

Even a first phone call just to introduce yourself and say that you are looking forward to having Jimmy in class this year can lay some positive groundwork for the future. We talk about additional ways to do this later in this chapter.

The fourth guideline for praise is *clean*. This is often a very challenging requirement for praise. The expectation that praise be clean is especially challenging for educators. Clean means a couple of different things.

One is that it is not clean praise if you are issuing it in order to get the student or parent to do something in the future. In other words, it is important to compliment students because their efforts are authentic, not just because you are hoping that they will do something different tomorrow. It is important to remind yourself of this quite regularly, because if you do not, you will be tempted to discontinue praising because you feel it "did not work." An example of this would be if you call a parent with praise for a less positive student for the effort he or she used on a science experiment in class that morning, and then later in the week the student is less than polite to you. Do not feel that these two events are linked. Oftentimes we take the less than positive approach of students very personally. Although our goal is to get them to be more productive, we need to be aware that more often their mood has much more to do with them and the way they feel about themselves than it does with you and how they are regarding you.

The second requirement for praise to be clean is a very challenging one for teachers and principals: It cannot include the word "but." If we are trying to compliment a student and say, "Billy did a good job on his math quiz yesterday, but . . . his science homework was done very poorly," the individual we hoped we were praising will very likely only remember the part after "but," which was a criticism. It is very unlikely that he or she will be able to recall the attempted compliment. If we really mean to praise someone, then it is important that we divide these two events. If we had stopped with, "Billy did a good job on his math quiz yesterday," then this could have been an authentic, specific, immediate, positive, and reinforcing event for this student (and help establish relations with the parent!). The other part of the comment, "his science homework was done very poorly" may have no need for immediacy. Tying these two together reduces or even eliminates the value of the praise.

The fifth descriptor of praise is *private*. Dr. Bissell believes that the vast majority of the time, praise needs to be given in private. I agree with this and would also say that when in doubt, you are always safe to praise someone in private. Calling the parent of a student not only helps cultivate positive relations with the parent, but it is a private and personal way to reinforce the student's behavior.

WHAT DO I SAY WHEN I
MAKE A POSITIVE PHONE CALL?

Getting down a particular approach to doing something that you are unfamiliar with or even uncomfortable with can be very helpful in building up your confidence to doing it. I guess I first learned this approach when I was going to call a girl up and ask her out for a date. I would write down what I would say and even a couple of other topics to bring up in case the conversation fizzled. Once I knew how I wanted to start the phone call it gave me more confidence in actually dialing the phone. This same thing can be true if we are not used to initiating positive contact with parents.

Positive or negative, I would always start all of my phone calls in the same manner. I also shared this approach with the teachers in my school and especially with new faculty members. Everyone can meld an approach that works best for them, but having a place to start can go a long way toward building our skills. I would start every phone contact, positive or negative, with this language: "Hi, Mrs. Johnson, this is Tom Walker, assistant principal up at Smith Junior High. I am sorry to bother you at work (or home), but...."

We will discuss delivering bad news in Part IV of this book, but for now, let's continue examining a dialogue appropriate for making positive contact with parents.

As a principal, making a phone call when I received a positive referral would go like this, "Hi, Mrs. Johnson, this is Tom Walker, assistant principal up at Smith Junior High. I am sorry to bother you at work, but I just wanted you to know that Mrs. Martin, Kenny's math teacher has been running around up here at school bragging on your son. She said that he got a B+ on his math quiz yesterday and that she was very proud of the hard work he put into preparing for that quiz." I would then go on to say that I had a chance to call Kenny into my office earlier today and congratulate him and let him know how much I appreciate his hard work. I would usually close the conversation by sharing with the parent that I am sorry that I interrupted his or her work, but I just wanted to let him/her know what Mrs. Martin had said about Kenny in her positive referral.

For teachers, we would recommend a similar approach. Again, start each phone call to parents with the same language. "Hi, Mrs. Johnson, this is Karen Martin, Kenny's homeroom teacher. I am sorry to bother you at work, but I just wanted to let you know that Kenny did an excellent job leading his group in the science experiment this morning. He was very organized, and I really appreciated his efforts. I wrote him a note on his grade sheet telling him how proud I was of his efforts and, again, I did not want to bother you, but I just wanted to let you know what an excellent job he did this morning in class. Have a good day."

Different people might have different approaches, but we want to be very consistent in the way we interact with parents. By having a specific approach with how we always initiate contact allows for a more level and diplomatic conversation regardless of what kind of news was shared.

One of the most powerful aspects of initiating the positive contact was what I received from the students the next day. One of the comments they would share most frequently was how excited their parents were and how much they appreciated it.

Do not ever underestimate the value of positive contact with parents. I could call them in September and if the next time I interacted with them was April, they would still remember and acknowledge how much it meant to them, even if my April contact was to inform them of a punishment.

You Mean I Got Something in the Mail Besides a bill?

In addition to the phone calls, a similar approach is to send positive postcards or letters home to parents about something good that their child accomplished. Many schools do this on a regular basis. We had postcards made that had a printed border around the outside in our school colors that said Wonderful!, Terrific!, Great Job!, or Way to Go! On the address side, our school name and motto was printed. Then any staff member could write something positive on the postcard regarding the student. Again, we would keep in mind the five things that help praise work.

We would address and mail them to the parents of the students. This is another way to not only reinforce positive student behavior, but also to enhance positive relations with all parents in the school. This may be doubly appropriate with students whose parents do not have phones.

I remember that when we first started sending the postcards I wondered if junior high kids even cared about this type of thing. However, I'll never forget that years after some students went through our school I could go into their homes, and every postcard they ever received from our staff was still prominently posted on the family refrigerator. And I do believe that having the parents think positive thoughts about you and your school every time they get out the milk is probably very beneficial in establishing the relationship that you would like.

As a teacher, if you are the only person in the school who is doing this, you may have to use standard postcard or generate a special letterhead on your computer that only you would use. As a principal, you could have these postcards printed up by the hundreds and regularly give them to everyone in the school—cooks, custodians, bus drivers, teachers, and other staff. It would even help promote this activity more if you could have office personnel or parent volunteers address the postcards for the staff so that it would be as easy as possible for the faculty. They could just turn in the postcards to the office, and then someone else would address the mailings.

The value of initiating positive contact can never be underestimated. Although it may be something that we are not familiar with, or maybe something that we used to do but have moved away from, there is no more effective way to build credibility with parents. And it is essential that we do this as often as possible with the students and parents that have the most potential for future negative interactions.

Making sure that you remind yourself to make positive phone calls and/or mail positive messages can be a challenge for everyone. We always find time for whatever is most important, so we just have to decide that this is that important. Writing it down in our lesson plan book or calendar is often a productive way to do this. I would write in my calendar to make two positive phone calls every Tuesday and send positive postcards every Friday. Of course, this not only helped nurture positive relations with students and parents, it also made me feel good!

YOU NEVER GET
A SECOND CHANCE

It is impossible to overestimate the goodwill that is generated by taking the time to make a positive first impression. This time and effort will be returned in a multitude of ways that will make your job easier and much more enjoyable.

6

LISTEN, LEARN, AND CULTIVATE

In several recent surveys of educational leaders, the one area in which many of them indicated that they would have liked to receive more training is interpersonal communication. Whether we are talking to a group of school administrators or a group of teachers, everybody seems to be increasingly recognizing the power of positive communication. The challenge arises when the individual or group of individuals we are communicating with is a difficult one. As everybody can attest to, it is far easier to communicate with a positive person than it is to communicate with somebody who is difficult.

However, the hallmark of greatness involves the educator's ability to effectively communicate with even the most difficult people. This communication, when handled in a productive manner, often has the power to diffuse even the most *difficult* situation by winning over perhaps the most *difficult* person. To do so, educators need to understand that relationships do not just happen automatically. Difficult people cannot become our allies or supporters simply because we want this to be so. Instead, positive relationships with parents must be cultivated. We are reminded again of Covey's urgency that we "seek first to understand, then to be understood." (Covey, 1990, p. 255) We can do this with parents when we listen to their concerns, learn as much as we can about their perspective, and then begin to cultivate a positive relationship.

This idea of listening, learning, and cultivating relationships really boils down to having effective communication skills. Too many educators think of communication with parents as being something they do when there is a problem. This is partly due to the fact that, as educators, we are all very busy people. It seems difficult to imagine having the time to communicate with parents when everything is going along well. As the best among us know, this is precisely the time when we ought to be communicating, particularly if our goal is to cultivate positive relationships with parents.

COMMUNICATING IN GOOD TIMES

The best, most effective educators are the ones who communicate with all stakeholders on a regular and consistent basis. Not only do they regularly communicate, but also they do so in a proactive manner. They understand that communication may be ineffective if it's always delivered as a reaction or a response to a problem. This communication takes place when things are going well in addition to when things are not going so well. The least effective educators, on the other hand, spend all of their communication time dealing with situations in which somebody did something wrong. These people seem to disappear during good times, only to reappear again when somebody has done something wrong. The effect this has on an already difficult person or in an already difficult situation can be very damaging. Yet again, it must be noted that the busy professional lives many educators experience cause them to be reactive in their communication with others. Proactivity is required if we are to communicate with parents and other school stakeholders on a regular and consistent basis.

Effective communication, we should know, must occur in good times as well as in bad times. If, for example, a principal is known to communicate with students, staff members, and parents only when there are problems, then there will be a negative impact felt on the overall culture of the school. The school, as we have too often seen, will become mired in a culture of negativity. The norm will fast become one in which people dread seeing the principal at all. This is due to the fact that the principal has earned the reputation of being the bearer of bad news. A parent, already harboring negative feelings about the school or a school-related situation, will instinctively enter into conversations with such a principal from a defensive or aggressive stance. Either way, the parent will not be open to hearing what the principal has to say if he/she already expects it to be negative.

The same can be said of every single staff member in a school. If teachers only send home notes when children are failing or misbehaving, for example, then parents will quickly begin to dread hearing from them. We know that the thought of a parent dreading to see a note with our handwriting on it or shuddering when they hear that we are on the other end of the telephone depresses us incredibly. We entered the field of education to make a positive difference in the lives of children. We imagine you feel the same way. Shouldn't we want people to be excited when they hear from us? Specific ways to make this excitement possible were discussed in Chapter 5. Utilizing those techniques is essential if we want to cultivate positive relationships.

The most respected, effective educators use varied forms of communication to regularly provide feedback to all stakeholders, especially parents. They contact parents with good news as often as they contact them with bad news. They use more formal means like regular newsletters or class web pages, as well as more casual ones like spontaneous telephone calls or conversations in the hallways. Though these educators do not hesitate to illustrate when something bad has happened or when something has been done incorrectly, they balance this with a healthy dose of positive communication. The result, more often than not, is a healthy relationship with parents. Developing and maintaining healthy relationships with parents is, therefore, vitally important to the success of any school. These healthy relationships come about through involvement and engagement of all parents. They do not come about in schools that alienate parents or communicate with them only in times of trouble. Here are three simple reasons why these healthy relationships are so important in the creation of positive school-home relationships:

♦ Students are more successful in school when their parents and school personnel work closely and cooperatively.

♦ Parents will be more supportive and willing to give educators the benefit of the doubt, even in stress-filled and emotional encounters, when there is a history of working together.

♦ Everyone in the schooling business (parents, teachers, administrators, and students) will benefit from two-way information sharing and collaborative problem solving. (McEwan, 1998b, p. 79)

Note the consistent theme in all three reasons: collaboration. Education can be a difficult enough business. It is so much more difficult when we attempt to perform our duties without collaborative, supportive relationships. Therefore, it makes no sense at all to fail to do all we can to collaborate with parents. As this section of the book has shown, communication is the key to building collaborative relationships.

WE'RE GLAD YOU'RE HERE

It is essential that we do everything within our power to make parents feel welcome in our schools. It is amazing to note, however, that many schools across the country blow the opportunity to do so immediately inside the front door of the school building. As an example, examine the policy that most schools must have nowadays that restricts visitor access by locking doors and forcing visitors to sign in at the main office before proceeding to another part of the school building. Though these measures may certainly be deemed necessary in the current environment, they still set a tone that we must work to overcome. We believe that the intended objective of these policies can be accomplished in a much friendlier and more welcoming manner than is currently done in many schools.

While these policies have become commonplace in our schools, the means by which they are announced and enforced differ from one another dramatically. In some schools, there are signs on the doors using language similar to the following: "Stop! All visitors must sign in at the office before proceeding further." Many of these announcements are on posters shaped and colored to resemble stop signs. Is that more effective than the following example? "Welcome to our school! We are so glad that you are here! We do ask that all visitors please sign in at the office upon entering." Which message has a friendlier tone? Which message is more likely to make you really feel welcome?

Now, some may argue that the forceful language in the first example is necessary. Without such forcefulness, people would not listen. We, however, maintain that individuals who would ignore a message that says, "Welcome to our school! We are so glad that you are here. We do ask that all visitors please sign in at the office upon entering," are also more likely to ignore a more forceful message. In the meantime, by using a forceful message, we have unintentionally made some of our more positive parents feel unwelcome in our school because of the rather unfriendly edict that greeted them. The odds are that the same people will report to the office no matter how the message is delivered. Furthermore, from a safety standpoint, our hope is that if somebody has entered the school building with the intent to harm someone, they will do more than just visit the office. Our hope is that they will confess to the harm they are intending to cause. In this regard, visiting the office does not by itself make the school safer. It does create a feeling of safety, which helps alleviate the stress of some of our parents.

Another point to consider is the impact a negative greeting can have on a parent who rarely comes to your school. Because we are in our school buildings every day and we understand and regularly witness all of the positive things that go on in the school, an unfriendly greeting posted on the door doesn't seem like such a big deal to us. In fact, many educators probably don't even notice these greetings on a regular basis. The parent who only ventures into your school once or twice a year is much more affected by these messages, though. This ought not be forgotten.

The kind of welcoming greeting we are speaking of here goes beyond the sign that welcomes visitors upon entering the school. The entire atmosphere of the school's entryway must be considered here. A sign with a cheerful greeting placed in a dark and dingy entryway will do less to make a parent feel welcome than would the same sign placed in a bright and cheery entryway. Though we believe that the whole school should be attractively decorated, it is extremely important that efforts be made to make at least the entryway attractive. A very good technique for accomplishing this task is to involve or empower your parent organization. In this way, not only will the entryway be kept neat, clean, and welcoming, but also the very population you seek to welcome will feel ownership for the project's success.

Again, school safety is a real concern that we all share. It is prudent that we implement policies that will make our schools safer for all children. In doing so, we must maintain common sense, though. Schools can be safe and friendly at the same time. The welcoming greeting can be written so as to proclaim the importance of safety, but it can also contain helpful directions to the office and a sense that we really are welcoming our visitors.

Celebrating cultural heritages, diverse careers, and hidden hobbies and talents is one more way to say to parents, "We're glad you're here." Regardless of your school's level, there are tremendous opportunities to welcome parents in to share some of their abilities and insights relative to their jobs or the ways in which their families celebrate holidays. Not only do these situations provide rich learning opportunities for your students, but they assist you in cultivating positive relationships with parents as you show them how much you want to learn from them.

THERE IS A TIME AND A
PLACE FOR ALL CONVERSATIONS

We all have our comfort zones. These comfort zones may be a location in the school building, a favorite chair, or a preferred seating posture. Regardless, every one of us has a place where we like to have conversations with parents. We all have mannerisms that we use to make us feel a degree of comfort in these conversations. What we sometimes fail to realize is that our comfort zone is often very different from the comfort zone of the parents we may be meeting with. By setting up the room before a parent conference in a way that makes us feel comfortable and in control, we often make the parent feel very uncomfortable. Without a doubt, this will lead a difficult person to become defensive and, perhaps, even more difficult.

I remember my first principalship vividly. In particular, I remember the new desk chair that I was given shortly after assuming the position. The chair was a very high, executive-looking one, and, though my office was small, sitting in that chair behind my large desk made me look more powerful and imposing than I had ever looked before. With this in mind, what do you suppose would have happened if I sat in that chair behind that desk for all the conferences and conversations that took place in my office? Would people have felt comfortable and at ease in speaking with me? Would I have been more likely to cultivate positive relationships with parents, or would I have further erected a wall that separated us?

There really is a time and a place for all conversations. There were times when the imposing look I could create sitting in my big chair served a purpose. The point of appearing confident and self-assured when dealing with a difficult or irrational person is elaborated on in the next chapter. This being said, though, 95+ percent of the interactions I had in my office took place with me sitting in a smaller chair facing an individual in the same size chair with no desk in between us. The equal playing field this position presented was vitally important in creating the kind of relationship that I always wished to foster.

The same idea exists in classrooms. When teachers invite parents in for conferences, it makes no sense for the teachers to sit in their desk chairs while the parent is squeezed into a student's chair. This is particularly so for teachers in the primary grades. Mrs. Rodriquez is far less comfortable sitting in her 6-year-old's chair, for example, than she would be if she sat facing you in the same adult-sized chair that you were sitting in. With the negative feelings that some parents harbor before they even enter our schools, why would we intentionally exacerbate these feelings with the way in which we furnish and arrange the room?

THE OWL DOESN'T JUST SCREECH

When I was growing up, there was a framed saying that my parents had hung in our house. Though I do not recall precisely where it hung, its message has made an indelible mark on me. It said:

> A wise old owl lived in an oak. The more he saw, the less he spoke. The less he spoke, the more he heard. Why can't we be like that old bird?

Heeding this message can help us a great deal, particularly when we deal with parents in difficult situations. Too often, we educators make the mistake of thinking that our main purpose is to solve problems. Sometimes, what we need to do is to look and listen. When we take the time to really listen, we can learn so much. When we learn, we are in a position to cultivate positive relationships. These positive relationships with parents will help us to achieve our mission so much more than negative relationships will. We must listen, learn, and cultivate. This will form the necessary foundation for dealing with difficult parents.

PART III

DEALING WITH DIFFICULT PARENTS: SOOTHING THE SAVAGE BEAST

7

NEVER LET 'EM
SEE YOU SWEAT

There is an old deodorant commercial that used the slogan, "Never let 'em see you sweat." The premise behind the advertising campaign was that in the rough-and-tumble business world sweating was a sure sign of defeat. If you were involved in heavy business negotiations, and the opposition saw that you were perspiring, they would somehow realize that they had gotten to you. Now, they could move in for the kill. This premise went beyond television commercials and has been consistently repeated in movies as well. The confident "good guy" never sweats. In fact, those who sweat have traditionally been depicted as weak, frightened, lying, and on the verge of collapse. One of our favorite movie scenes comes from *Broadcast News* and finds Albert Brooks sweating profusely during his big break as a news broadcaster. The pressure of being an anchorman, much like the pressure of dealing with a difficult parent, was apparently too much for him to handle.

Borrowing from this contemporary media view of perspiring, it is important that when dealing with a difficult parent, you never let 'em see you sweat. This is to say that as long as you appear confident and self-assured, even the most difficult parent's anger will be somewhat diffused. As soon as your body language indicates that you are unnerved, however, then the offensive onslaught of a difficult parent may become pronounced. This will obviously put you at a distinct disadvantage.

What happens when you are a bit unnerved, though? How do you prevent yourself from sweating—either literally or figuratively? What if the difficult parent's anger really has taken you by surprise and made you nervous? By understanding a few

77

simple techniques, you can appear confident. The appearance of being self-assured will pay huge dividends in the long run.

LOWER YOUR VOICE

If you think back to times when you were nervous, one of the places that this nervousness may have revealed itself is in the tone of your voice. When we are very nervous, there is a shaky sound to our voice. We swallow a lot and our voice trembles as if puberty has descended upon us once again. These vocal intonations are obviously more pronounced when our voice is loudest. Therefore, to compensate for the shakiness, we simply lower the volume of our voice. Subtleties, such as a shaky quality, become much more difficult to realize at this point.

The lower vocal volume gives us another benefit, as well. Consider this illustration that I use when speaking to a group of teachers about classroom management. I usually ask the group to tell me some of the techniques they use for quieting an unruly group of students. Invariably, through the wide range of responses I receive, somebody in the audience says, "I lower my voice until the only way that the students can hear me is to quiet down themselves." Usually, this leads others to recount tales of when they employed the same technique and received similar results. In fact, before long, many in the group begin realizing that this is among the best techniques for getting a roomful of noisy children to be quiet again. The fact is that many times a person who is speaking loudly or boisterously only realizes how ridiculous they sound when they have an opportunity to compare themselves with somebody else's quiet voice. At this point, their loudness becomes much more apparent and they begin to feel a bit self-conscious.

So, if a very angry parent arrived at my classroom or office door unexpectedly and began yelling, or at least speaking with an exceptionally loud voice, I would welcome him/her with the quietest voice I could muster. Many times, due to the fact that I was not expecting the parent, I may have been a bit unnerved. The quiet tone I used to communicate served two very important purposes for me, though:

1. It hid the nervous, shaky sound in my voice that might have put the angry parent at an advantage.

2. It served to quiet the angry parent's voice, as it showed him/her just how loud and boisterous he/she was being.

INCREASE YOUR MOVEMENT

Another trademark of a nervous, unsure person involves uncontrolled body movements like wobbling knees and shaking hands. While it was very rare for a difficult parent to make me feel this degree of nervousness, there were times when it did occur. Telling myself not to be nervous and to stop shaking only seemed to make the problem worse. Therefore, I *increased* many of my other body movements to make these uncontrollable ones less obvious. This increase in motion made it appear as though I was trying to multitask because I was such a busy person. While listening to the parent I would put things away that were lying on my desk, or I would pace behind the desk clasping my hands as if I were working through an important idea in my head. If these motions seemed inappropriate for the moment, I might jot down a note or just tap my pencil. While these movements may have appeared rude and uncaring if I took them to an extreme, I always felt that it was better than the alternative of appearing to be a nervous person with wobbling knees or shaking hands. Remember, the goal here is to never let 'em see you sweat.

Just as in the case of lowering my voice, there was an added, unplanned benefit to all of this movement. Oftentimes, my movement caused the parent to become nervous or uneasy. Though unintentional, I had turned the tables on the difficult parent and started them on a path of nervous behavior. As the parent followed my actions while I moved around the room, I would gain some self-confidence. This, in turn, would allow me to gradually stop moving, assume my position in my big chair behind my desk, and regain control of a conversation that clearly began with me on the defensive.

CLOSE THE GAP

Think for a moment of a loud, boisterous playground bully that you have dealt with before. This may be a student who is currently in your school, or it may be a bully that you had the displeasure of dealing with when you were a child. Regardless, think of the loudest, most threatening bully you can imagine. What happened whenever this bully started bellowing? My guess is that everybody backed away a few steps. This is a natural reaction and one that the loud, boisterous person often wants you to exhibit. Therefore, another technique to consider when dealing with an angry parent who is acting this way is to close the gap and move a bit closer in proximity to the angry person.

This change in proximity must be done very calmly, while you are exhibiting open body language. It should be subtle, but focused on the goal of moving you even closer to the other person, as unnatural as that may feel.

THE EYES HAVE IT

A fourth technique in preventing difficult parents from seeing you sweat involves forcing yourself to look the difficult parent straight in the eye. Though difficult at first, particularly if you have been taken by surprise, looking a person directly in the eye gives you an air of self-confidence and self-assurance. More often than not, this technique quickly turned things in my favor and put me in control of the conversation. As stated earlier, we need to remember that many of our most difficult parents had many of their own negative experiences when they were students. As a result, many of them are much more intimidated by being in a school facility than they would initially like us to believe. Though this is certainly no cause for celebration and is actually a truth that we should hope to change, we need to understand the role it plays in the attitude parents often bring with them to school. Their anger, or the inherent need to protect their child from perceived harm, may lead them to your school with an air of confidence, but this confidence can quickly give way to a feeling of nervousness or apprehension if you employ the right techniques. Looking the parent squarely in the eye is one such technique. By looking an angry parent in the eye, we can convey a certain degree of understanding. More often than not, this will reduce the level of their anger. We can also show the parent that we are surprised by what they are telling us. Doing this with our eyes can help the parent to see that comments such as theirs are unusual or unexpected. This may even cause the angry parent to calm down somewhat. If nothing else, looking a parent squarely in the eye shows the parent that you are listening. As we are well aware, this is often the only thing the difficult parent wants from us.

In some ways, the four techniques explained in previous sections may appear to be merely mind games that we play in difficult situations. Upon closer examination, they are really much more, though. They are proven strategies that will often prevent you from appearing to be nervous or weak. Remember, the purpose of all of this is to improve relationships with parents for the benefit of our students. A parent who comes into the school building with a problem and encounters a teacher or a principal who appears nervous at worst and uneasy at best is probably not a parent who is going to feel confident that his/her child's school is guided by strong, confident educators. If we, as educators but not trained mediators, need to employ some calculated strategies to appear more confident, then are we really doing something bad?

Another point to consider is that the whole reason for working toward developing positive relationships with all parents is so that all children will succeed. Therefore, even if we are not concerned with appearing to be overly strong or confident, we ought to at least be concerned with maintaining positive and productive conversations with parents. A difficult parent who arrives at the school feeling angry is not a parent that we can enjoy a rational, productive conversation with. If we must employ some well-planned techniques to calm this parent down so that we may "get down to business," then we are certainly behaving in a manner that brings us closer to the achievement of our goal—namely, positive and productive relationships with parents for their children's benefit.

Finally, consider the benefits that these communication methods can bring you in terms of the perception of you by the rest of the school community. When I was a principal, it was always important to me for my staff to see me as a leader. I appeared to be much more of a leader when I was not nervous or afraid of confrontation. This is not to say that a leader should be fearless and arrogant. No, the best leaders are human leaders, and with this human element comes the ability to feel and show emotions. However, when parents arrived at my school angry about what they perceived one of my teachers to have done, it was always important that I did not appear to be frightened to have a discussion with them. The teacher in question, even if he or she had done something that he/she should not have done, needed to see that my initial assumption was that the parent must be mistaken, or at least must have misunderstood something. Being nervous or afraid simply would not communicate this message. What it might communicate is my uncertainty about whether or not the teacher may have really done something wrong.

The same concept applied when I was a teacher. Because teachers are educational leaders as well, I always wanted to appear confident and in control. Again, it was never imperative that I appeared to know all the answers, but it was important that students, colleagues, parents, and all other school stakeholders knew that I was confident in my abilities. Intimidating parents, angry because of a one-sided story they had heard, entered my classroom from time to time. I knew then that it was important to my success that I not let these parents believe that I was frightened, uneasy, or intimidated.

Again, it really doesn't matter what your position is in a school. If difficult parents are able to intimidate you, not only do you risk losing the respect of those around you, but also you increase the odds that you will cave in to the difficult parents and yield to their requests. Other parents who see this happen may become very upset and think that bullying and intimidating you are ways to get what they want. The squeaky wheel should not always get the grease. It's not only important that difficult parents shouldn't see you sweat, but parents watching from the outside shouldn't either.

The techniques and behaviors discussed in this chapter remain just as effective regardless of what your position is in a school. While I employed them more as a principal than I did when I was teaching, this was due mostly to the fact that I encountered more difficult parents while I was a principal. However, and I am certain most readers will agree, teachers also encounter their share of difficult parents who arrive at the classroom door angry and unannounced. Even if the teacher is right and the parent misunderstands an issue that may have arisen at school, the teacher is apt to get nervous when the parent storms into the classroom screaming. Remembering the methods described in this chapter will not automatically lead the educator to a peaceful conversation filled with mutual growth and understanding, but it will accomplish one important step toward this noble goal. It will make it so that you never let 'em see you sweat. As movies and television have told us before, this is half of the battle.

8

WHAT IF THE PARENT IS RIGHT?

One of the greatest difficulties administrators encounter is when a parent calls to complain about a teacher's alleged inappropriate behavior, and it turns out that the parent is right. These situations do not necessarily need to involve allegations of gross misconduct on the teacher's part. Instead, they can be simple situations like a miscalculated grade or a misplaced student assignment. The reason for the difficulty has little to do with the error that was made. It has a great deal to do, however, with the challenge of supporting the teacher while acknowledging that the parent's complaint has merit.

From a teacher's perspective, the situations suggested above also present a challenge. When parents call on the telephone or makes a surprise visit to the classroom to report their perception of a problem, more often than not they are missing some facts. As a result, the perception they arrived at is often misguided. Sometimes, however, they are right. Sometimes, the wrong that the parents perceive to have occurred actually did occur. In these difficult times, what's an educator to do?

Again, although the scope of the issue may be different if you are a principal than if you are a teacher, the approaches for responding to these parents are very similar. Though it sounds so simple and cliched, honesty is always the best policy. In dealing with difficult parents, you should never feel the need to always be right. Never believe that your leadership skills or educational qualifications hinge, even to a slight degree, on showing difficult parents that their perception of a situation is incorrect. It should never be about winning or losing. It should be about arriving at a common understanding and doing so in an agreeable productive manner.

So, whether thinking back to my days as a teacher or to those I spent as a principal, I always remained mindful of the fact that my interactions with difficult parents were designed to get us both on the proverbial same page. Perhaps more significantly, I really wanted to get us there in an agreeable manner with the hope that it would lessen any future difficulties. It was perfectly okay for the parents to be right. In fact, I was quick to point out how much I appreciated the parents' ability to uncover the facts about issues and to present them to me in a way that would expedite the correction of any wrongdoing. The key in all of these situations was to appreciate the parents for bringing issues to my attention and to quickly inform them that the wrong that was committed was not done so intentionally. Then, in all cases, I made sure that I affirmed the parents for presenting the issue in a rational, understanding manner, even if that was not at all the manner in which they actually presented it. Consider this example as an illustration:

THE INCORRECT GRADE

All teachers, whether they use electronic grading systems or hand calculations, run the risk of making the occasional grading error. While these errors are often insignificant, and while we all have no problem acknowledging and then correcting them, they can send the already difficult parents into a fit. No sooner does the student bring the paper that has been incorrectly scored home, then the parents arrive at the classroom demanding that justice be served. As discussed in the previous chapter, it is important that the angry parents not see you sweat. Employing the techniques from Chapter 7, you should welcome the parents into the room; acknowledge their feelings with a comment like, "Gee, Mrs. Jones, you seem so upset. Please come in so I can help you with your problem," and then let them explain the error. At this point, you have shown the parents that you are not defensive, you have left open the door that maybe they are correct, and you have subtly pointed out that the parents' behavior is not at present as rational as yours.

It is wise and prudent to look next at the grade in question and determine if, in fact, an error was made. Assuming it was, you should thank the parents for pointing it out, quickly correct it, and close with a comment like, "Caring parents like you are exactly what our schools need more of. Thank you for pointing this out to me so that I could correct it. Your cooperative nature is exactly what will help us work as a team for the benefit of your child." In doing so, you have lost no dignity, you have shown the parents that you are human and, consequently, make mistakes, and you have illustrated for them how agreeably such issues can be resolved.

SORRY SEEMS TO BE THE HARDEST WORD

There is one more very significant step that you should employ when a parent is right. If the parent is upset about something that you have done wrong, you should apologize. The same is true whether you did something wrong, or if the complaint is about somebody else on the staff. By apologizing, particularly in the cases where the issue involves something somebody else did, you are not necessarily admitting any guilt or acknowledging a wrongdoing. You don't have to be sorry that a staff member did something that a parent alleges he or she did. You can simply be sorry that the parent perceives that the event happened and is upset about it. Then, you can begin uncovering the facts to determine if things transpired exactly as the parent says they did. If so, be secure enough to apologize again. When parents recognize that you are sorry when you do things incorrectly, it is amazing how willing they become to forgive you. When you refuse to ever acknowledge that you, or anybody else in your school, is capable of doing wrong, then many parents go on a mission to prove just how wrong you actually are. The importance of saying that you are sorry is explored in even greater depth in Chapter 9.

SOMETIMES IT'S
IMPORTANT TO BE FIRST

If you or somebody you supervise makes a mistake that could lead to parents becoming upset and calling you to complain, call the parents first. Though we may initially dread the idea and fear that we are going to receive an earful, the pain this saves in the long run can be tremendous. In all times of discomfort, it is usually a good idea to be proactive. By contacting parents who you know are upset before they contact you, a great deal of their anger can be diffused. If, instead, we hide our heads in the sand and hope that the parents won't call us, then nine times out of ten all we do is give the parents more time to become even angrier.

I can recall one time several years ago when I was in a terrible hurry (as I usually am), and I stopped to pick up a dry cleaning order on the way home. I pulled into the parking lot where the dry cleaner was located and bolted from my car to pick up my order. The clerk who greeted me was very pleasant, handed me several items on hangers, took my money, and wished me a good day. Grabbing the hangers, I hurried to my car and headed home. When I got home and was putting the clothing in my closet, I noticed that one of my shirts was missing. My immediate thought was, "That stupid clerk! How could he forget to give me all of my clothes? I'll bet he remembered to charge me for everything, though!"

As I walked toward the telephone to call and complain, reading the receipt on the way, I noticed that the red light on the answering machine was lit, indicating that I had received a message. I pressed the "play" button and was surprised to hear, "Hi, this is Jason from Crown Dry Cleaners. Look, I'm really sorry, but I forgot to give you one of the shirts you had paid for. It's no excuse, but we had been so busy today that I must have mixed it up with an incoming order. For your trouble and because we really appreciate your business, the manager has authorized me to offer to clean your next five shirts free. You can pick this one up at your convenience. Again, I'm really sorry." Do you know how I felt after listening to that? I felt pretty stupid, to tell you the truth. After all, everybody makes mistakes. I was embarrassed that I even got angry in the first place.

Think of how differently this all might have turned out if Jason had not called me. I would have called him, probably behaving in a manner that I would later be ashamed of. Maybe he would have become defensive, and the outcome would have been entirely different. At best, he would have let me blow off steam, but made the same offer to clean the next five shirts for free. Then, I would have felt guilty for acting the way I did, and both of us would have had a bad day. Because he proactively acknowledged his simple mistake, though, this story had a happy ending.

This same concept can be applied to our dealings with parents. Sometimes, we do make mistakes. Sometimes, particularly with the difficult ones, the parents become angry. In all cases, we gain nothing by becoming defensive and insisting that we did nothing wrong. When we are honest, when we admit our mistakes, when we apologize for the trouble they may have caused, and when we are proactive, then a parent who is right gives us the opportunity to be right also.

9

THE BEST WAY TO GET IN THE LAST WORD...

There is an old saying that the best way to get in the last word is to apologize. This saying may be true in a great number of settings, but it may be most applicable and effective in working with difficult parents. We have found that the single best defuser in any situation is to apologize. Many educators do this. However, the specific wording that we use is essential because it can allow us to calm the waters and yet retain our dignity. It is very difficult to say, "I was wrong...." It is even more difficult to say that when it is not true. But there is one way we can approach all situations that will help satisfy even the most aggressive parents while at the same time allowing us to be honest in our approach. Let's take a look at this method.

I Am Sorry That Happened

It is amazing how one approach can apply to a myriad of situations, whether the situation is between an educator and a student, between two teachers, an administrator-teacher struggle, or any challenging situation involving a parent. Being able to say, "I am sorry that happened," is universally applicable language. Imagine the following scenario (though it probably will not take much imagining!).

You receive a phone call at night from an irate parent who is a consistent pain in the neck (or even lower). The parent belligerently exclaims that his/her son, David, was being picked on in the hallway (or at recess, in the locker room, etc.) at school that day, and nobody did anything about it. You ask the parent to share a little more information, and he or she continues to share details that apparently a couple of other boys shoved

David against the wall and were threatening him and calling him names. Obviously, you know little more about the situation than what the parent has just shared with you. However, you can rely on your apology wording.

You can say, "Mrs. Smith, I am sorry that happened. I appreciate you calling to share this information, and I will make sure I look into it tomorrow, and I will also visit with David to see if he has any more details to share. I will also make sure that I visit with the other boys that were involved, but I sure am sorry that happened."

Examine closely what you said. You did not assume any responsibility for the incident, but you still expressed that you were sorry that it happened. You might be thinking to yourself right now, "I am not sorry that it happened, that is a lie." Well, not if you add a second part to the statement. With the rudest and most unpleasant parents to work with, I say verbally, "I am sure sorry that happened." However, *to myself* I add, "...otherwise I wouldn't be visiting with you right now!" And, that is the truth. With our most challenging parents we would schedule a root canal in lieu of meeting with them if we could.

And, truth be told, regardless of what occurred, now that you have to spend even more time dealing with them, aren't you truly sorry that it happened? This perspective was amazingly refreshing to me and allowed me to help them feel that I was seeing things from their point of view while allowing me to retain my dignity in the situation.

It is also essential to make sure that we do use a sympathetic tone and manner. As in all settings, if we allow rudeness, arrogance, impatience, or sarcasm to drip into our voice, then we have generally fanned the flames in a very negative way.

This exact same approach is appropriate in a face-to-face setting. If parents march into your office or classroom and share any situation that is of concern to them regarding their child, stating that you are sorry that it happened may be very beneficial. As a principal defending a teacher, this is also a productive approach. You are not blaming staff members, or necessarily defending them, but you are truly sorry that the situation occurred. Getting parents calmed down and into a listening mode is an important step toward developing an amicable solution to their concerns.

Even if you initiate the conversation, this same tool is appropriate. If I have to call parents and tell them that their daughter was cheating on a test or is being held after school, regardless of the circumstance, I really am sorry that it happened. This attitude also helps develop some common ground with parents. Because, regardless of their disposition, they are probably sorry that it happened, also. And, in any type of negotiation, establishing some commonalities is an important step to settling the issue in a way that both sides can live with.

AN EAR, NOT AN ANSWER

Often, even irate parents want someone to listen to them more than they want someone to solve their problems. They may live in an environment where they feel no one listens. Their work may not be of a structure that allows them to share their feelings, perspectives, or thoughts. And, honestly, with many of the most challenging parents that we work with, their children probably don't listen too well to them either. Thus, if we can help them feel that we are on their side and that we are attempting to see things from their point of view, it may go a long way to calming them down and building up a level of trust with them that may serve us well in the future.

Sharing with people, "I am sorry that happened," can help us achieve many of these goals, and it is just as appropriate to say to the nicest parents in the school as to the ones that we least look forward to working with. Practicing this language in many situations outside as well as inside school can help us to use it effectively during more stressful or confrontational settings involving parents.

10

Do You feel Defensive? If so, Something Is Wrong

One of our favorite sayings is that educators should never be defensive, *and* they should never be offensive. If we are truly caring people, then as teachers, principals, and superintendents, we should never be defensive when we deal with parents. We might feel awkward, uncomfortable, intimidated, but we should not feel *defensive*. If we are making all of our decisions based on what is best for students, then this defensiveness should not be occurring. If we do feel defensive, then it is probably because we, or someone we are attempting to support, has done something wrong.

If we are wrong, then it is essential that we apologize for our errors and then work diligently to not have that incident occur again. In this chapter, we discuss the situation in which the parent is wrong and we are right. However, being in touch with our feelings can help us to correct things before we put ourselves in the position of having to defend our actions. Let's take a look at a couple of examples.

RULES THAT MAKE NO SENSE

We truly believe that you do not control anyone's behavior by rules. We believe that everyone knows what the "rules" in life are and attempting to effect inappropriate behaviors by rules makes no sense. It is sort of like feeling the need to post a *No Smoking!* sign in the boys bathroom at school. Believe me, they all know they should not be smoking, it is just that the irresponsible students choose to do it anyhow. It is sort of like posting a *Shoplifters Will Be Prosecuted!* sign in a store. Trust me, the people who might shoplift know it is wrong—that is why they make sure no one is looking.

Well, in education, sometimes we do these same things. We attempt to hide behind rules. I was as guilty as anyone. I remember my first year as a seventh grade math teacher. I did not want to have to mess with students turning in assignments late, leaving class to go to their lockers, and so forth. And, for my own personal convenience, I did not want to have to grade late papers anyhow.

So I decided to have a rule that if you did not have your assignment with you in class, you would receive a zero on it. Boy, that made sense to me. As a matter of fact, for about the first third of the year it seemed to be a pretty good rule. Not too many students forgot their work and the ones that did were fairly irresponsible ones who probably did poorly on the assignment anyway. And realistically, most of the students who forgot their work weren't going to be competing for valedictorian anyhow.

I could also rationalize this rule by thinking that I was teaching responsibility to irresponsible seventh grade students. And, I gave enough different assignments that generally missing any one homework grade probably wasn't too significant in terms of a grade. But then, something happened. One of the nicest girls in the class, a hyperresponsible, straight-A student, forgot the most important assignment of the year. Not only was this a major assignment, but it was large enough that it would reduce her quarter grade dramatically and even impact her semester grade. Yikes! She had it done, but in a hurry to not be late to class, (she also had perfect attendance as well as no tardies for the year) she left her work in her locker. To make matters even worse, her locker was just outside the door of the classroom.

Well, I can guarantee you that if I gave her a zero and her parents called me out of concern I would have felt very defensive. And the reason? The reason I would have felt defensive was because it was a silly rule to begin with. The impact, by chance, on this one student was so much greater than the impact on others who had missed minor assignments. When I realized how defensive I felt, I knew I had to change the rule and make amends with previous students who I had wronged.

Though it is nice to teach students lessons in responsibility, I guess maybe it is even more important to teach them lessons in empathy.

YOU CAN'T MAKE SENSE
OUT OF NO SENSE

Another example of being in touch with your feelings occurred when I was a first-year varsity basketball coach. We were having practice over the week between Christmas and New Year's Day. The day after Christmas we had practice, and two of my players were not there. They had not let me know they would be absent, they were just skipping practice. So, I did the all too common thing. I punished the players who were there by having them run dozens of extra sprints. This is a traditional approach still used by some coaches. The purpose of this idea is to cause those angry players who were there and were disciplined to in turn "punish" the guilty absent players. They feel that this type of peer pressure is one way to get others to alter their behaviors.

You know what? You don't have to be a genius to know that there is something wrong with this approach. Though I miraculously did not hear from any parents, I still realized that this was a silly thing to do. The only reason I did it is because that is what other coaches had done. I guess the other lesson that I would have taught the team was that if you hear of a player who is going to skip practice, you had better go ahead and skip practice, too!

Being sensitive to these inappropriate approaches can allow us as educators to avoid or minimize situations in which we have strong feelings of defensiveness. Just being aware of our emotions and being in touch with them can help us to establish reasonable guides and expectations for student behavior.

WHY DIDN'T I KNOW?

Being in touch with these defensive feelings is applicable to all educators when we fail to contact parents with information that is important. This is especially true if it is a situation we may have to deal with at a later point. If we get involved earlier, there may be less baggage or pent up emotions that would prevent us from being as productive as we would like. A common scenario is when we have to call parents over minor offenses that have reached their limit. Here is an example:

> As principals, if a teacher regularly sends students to the office with a note that says, "This is the fifth time in the last two weeks Jimmy has come to class without a pencil," we will probably make an initial effort to support this staff member. We may decide to punish this student, call their parent, and share the consequences. If we call the student's mother and share with her that her son is being given detention because this is the fifth time he has come to class without a pencil we are likely to get this reaction from his mom: "Why didn't I know?"

As principals, we feel defensive because we realize that the mother is right. A rule of thumb we have for all educators applies equally to people in more formal educational leadership roles. That is, that we should never feel defensive. If we do, it may be because we or someone in our school is doing something wrong. In this case, the teacher was doing something inappropriate, so we felt defensive when we were attempting to support her.

Asking and expecting staff to contact the parent *before* the student is sent to the office is an appropriate guideline. Realizing that some of the teachers may not regularly contact parents, providing them with some role modeling may be very appropriate. Explain that the call from the teacher is more effective because it is asking for the parent's assistance, not setting up a negative first contact regarding a punishment. The teacher could contact the parent and say, "Mrs. Johnson, I was wondering if I could get your help with something? Jimmy has not brought a pencil to class three times in the last week. I was not sure if you were aware of this, but I wanted to request your assistance before he ends up falling behind in class or before the office has to get involved. Could I get your help in visiting with him and making sure that he leaves for school prepared? Your assistance would greatly be appreciated."

Few parents would not agree to help. If the first contact is made in the form of a request for assistance, prior to their son or daughter being in "trouble," this is a very relationship-building contact. Now, I realize that a few parents will not follow through, and at some point the office may be involved. However, the difference is, at that time, rather than the principal feeling defensive because the parents "did not know," the parents will be the ones feeling on the spot because they did not follow through on their word. The point is not to make the parents feel defensive, but to make sure the educators are not backpedaling. Once this expectation is established, the teachers who do make this initial contact will end up preventing many office referrals.

This same scenario applies equally to all classroom teachers. If the first contact with parents can be to call and ask for their help, we may be able to avoid situations where parents ask us why they did not know earlier and then we feel the need to defend our actions. Instead, using a proactive interaction allows us and the parents to be on the same side. Consider this: When you share with the parent that you do not want Jimmy to fall behind in his work, does the parent want Jimmy to fall behind? Of course not. When you share that you do not want to have to get the office involved, do Jimmy's parents want to get the office involved? Of course not. Thus your relationship has started out on a positive note involving things that you and they agree on.

Taking time to reflect on our feelings can help us to be more effective in developing guidelines and expectations that are appropriate for our students, classrooms, and schools. Understanding the long-range benefit of dramatically reducing the frequency with which we feel that we are behind the eight-ball can allow us to view our jobs and our contact with parents in a more positive and productive light.

PART IV

DEALING WITH PARENTS IN DIFFICULT SITUATIONS

11

DELIVERING BAD NEWS— HEY, I'M JUST THE MESSENGER!

It is never any fun to be the bearer of bad news. Few of us ever look forward to ruining someone's day or potentially having to deal with the emotion of the recipient's reaction. And, as educators, some of us may be a little hesitant simply because of past experiences we have had or because of negative situations others may have described for us. Additionally, we may be having to contact or work with a parent who has a less than favorable reputation and that may add to our trepidation. In this chapter, we will focus on methods, tips, language, and approaches that can help us to most successfully tread these troubled waters.

THE WORSE THE NEWS, THE MORE EFFORT WE USE

Sometimes we have to deliver bad news when the parent contacts us or catches us unprepared. Many of the techniques we describe in this chapter and others in this section are very appropriate in all circumstances, including a parent-initiated contact. But, typically, the ball is in our court in terms of having to initiate that contact in some fashion. One of the first standards we should establish is that *the worse the news, the more thought and effort we need to put into delivering it*. As difficult as it may be, it is very important that we make personal contact when we have negative news to share with a parent. And, the more challenging the parent is, the more effort we must put forward.

It is essential that we seldom, if ever, deliver bad news in writing. Most of the time if we send notes home with students it is for our convenience or because it is easier for us in the short term than having to deal with a parent on the phone or in person. And, we know that a certain percentage of parents may not have home phones, but generally we should always make personal contact when delivering bad news.

One reason for this is very selfish. If you send a note home to difficult parents, your level of concern remains. You are not sure if they will be upset. And if they are, you may even imagine them showing up at your classroom or office unannounced in a fit of rage. Thus, potentially, your level of discomfort may continue indefinitely. Also, if they do call or drop in unexpectedly, you may be less prepared for them than if you were in charge of the contact. The final reason, and we will discuss this further in the chapter, is that if students carry notes home, they get to share their point of view with the parents before you do. Even if the note is mailed or delivered in a hermetically sealed envelope, they will still get to share their side of the story before you do. And, especially if it involves some type of misbehavior on their part, there is a *slight* chance that their version may be different than yours. And, with our most challenging students and their difficult parents, the kids usually know how to push the parents' buttons. If they didn't, then the student would generally not be so challenging.

THE PHONE IS OUR BEST FRIEND...
UNLESS IT IS RINGING

Probably the most effective and convenient way to contact a parent with bad news is using the phone. I always want to contact the parents if at all possible *before* the student has a chance to visit with them. This is especially true with the most difficult of parents in discipline situations. If students share their story first, then often we are in a defensive mode when we finally do reach the parents. They already have a viewpoint, and now we have to work to alter it. Now, we are very aware that many of our parents know of their child's willingness to bend the truth. However, this book is focused on dealing with our *most difficult* parents and difficult situations. These situations may be the ones in which we can rely on the student's honesty the least.

We also believe that we need to develop a consistent approach when contacting any parent for any reason. Each phone call, whether it be for a positive stroke or discussing a troubling situation should start out the same. We do not want parents to develop a negative mindset simply because of our first words or tone. Thus, we would recommend developing a structure that you start all calls with. If you will recall the wording for the positive phone calls discussed in Chapter 5, you will notice that we would start every parental contact in the same manner. Additionally, we need to use the same level, relaxed, and confident voice in all situations. Again, if we can practice our parental contacts by delivering good news, it can help us refine the specific wording and tone that we want to use in all phone conversations with family members. Here is an example of a potential script for delivering bad news:

> Hi, Mrs. Johnson, this is Tom Walker, assistant principal up at Smith Junior High. I am sorry to bother you at work (or home, depending on where I called), but today Kenny tripped a girl in the hallway and as a result he will receive two hours detention.

If I did not contact the parent before the student did, I would also add something to the effect of:

> Hi, Mrs. Johnson, this is Tom Walker, assistant principal up at Smith Junior High. I am sorry to bother you at work (or home, depending on where I called), and I do not know if Kenny shared this with you or not, but today Kenny tripped a girl in the hallway and as a result he will receive two hours detention.

By doing this I could gather information of what the student told his or her parent. Additionally, I would always want to shift the focus of the conversation to the future. Regardless of whether the student, parent, and you agree on what happened or the consequences, we all do want to make sure it does not happen again. Chapter 14 provides great detail on language and ways to help shift to a future focus. This is especially valuable in delivering bad news. Additionally, Chapter 12 helps us develop a way to get the parent to support our decision, and Chapter 13 provides some tools if they say we are not being fair.

HE NEVER LIES TO US!

I was always amazed at the number of parents who will respond to a difference between the student's story and the teacher/principal version by saying, "My son/daughter never lies to me!"

Again, as professional educators, we do not ever argue. Parents who respond like that are likely to be ready to argue. Instead of settling in a tit-for-tat discussion, treat them as though they were telling the truth and bring up a past inappropriate behavior by the student. In other words, assume that child does tell their parent everything. This can allow a shift away from the disputed incident and put you in more control of the situation. Rather than getting into a detailed discussion about whether or not it was really Jimmy talking in class inappropriately today, I would respond, without using sarcasm (though believe me, it was tempting) by saying:

> It sounds like you all have a very rare and special relationship. The fact that he never, ever lies to you is a tribute to both of you. Mrs. Smith, what did you think when Jimmy shared with you that he had to have his seat changed in the classroom *last Monday* because of throwing paper?

Often this will accomplish two goals. One is that it will at least temporarily move the conversation from a point that the parents dispute and feel very empowered to argue about to one that they may not have any knowledge of. It also tempers their insistence that "my son tells me everything." If you do this in a very professional and calm manner, you can typically move the parents back to the issue at hand. Assuming that their child does not really disclose everything to them, they may be in more of a mindset to be reasonable.

YOUR HONOR, I OBJECT

Though some of our challenging parents (and students) will want to act like lawyers, keep in mind that when we contact the family members we want to limit the amount of detail that we go into. This is doubly true with the people who will most want to pick apart every single action that we did while attempting to avoid any focus on the actions that their child did. This may not be easy to accomplish, but again, shifting the focus to the future can help with this. To center on the future, you can say, for example, "Mrs. Jones what do you think we can do to help avoid this type of situation in the future?" or "Mr. Smith would you please visit with Jennifer tonight and discuss alternative behaviors that she could choose in the future?"

This language helps us to avoid a Columbo-like recreation of the events. It also helps empower parents by giving them something to center on that they can control. And finally, it helps us to focus on the one thing that we all agree on, and that is that we do not want this to occur in the future.

BE AWARE OF WHAT
YOU DON'T KNOW

When I was an assistant principal dealing with discipline, many times I found myself talking with parents about issues that I did not observe firsthand. Regardless, I still had to figure out a way to work effectively with the situation. One way that worked was to be honest with the parent. I would often say, "One of the tough things about this situation, Mr. Martinez, is that for the two people talking right now, neither one of us was there." This would allow me to focus on what we did have control over. We could then center on the "what can we do to make sure this does not occur again" conversation.

If the parents were very belligerent, then I would shift the conversation to something that I did know about. For example, if parents insisted that this teacher was picking on their son and that their child was wrongly sent to the office, I would steer the dialogue from something I did not have first hand knowledge of to something that I *did* have personal awareness of. The conversation may take a turn in this direction:

> One of the tough things about this situation, Mr. Martinez, is that for the two people talking right now, neither one of us was there. And, obviously, neither one of use can sort out exactly what did occur. However, I want to share with you what I saw your son do in Mrs. Martin's class last Wednesday. I saw him out of his seat, disrupting other students, throwing his pencil at someone else, and poking at three students with scissors. And Mrs. Martin did not send him to the office that day. You need to know I thought his behavior was so inappropriate that she should have. However, if today his behavior was so bad that she did send him to the office, it only makes me shudder to think exactly what his behavior was today.

What I was doing with this conversation was reestablishing control of the discussion. Rather than focusing on something that I did not have firsthand knowledge about (today's behavior), I centered on something that I did observe that was inappropriate. Not only did this take the focus off of this disputed situation, it also defended the teacher by indicating that she was more tolerant and fair than I would have been.

Again, you need to be selective in using this approach, but in very challenging situations this is a powerful tool. The same thing can occur with a classroom teacher. You could contact parents regarding their child bullying other students. Your contact this time may be about a reported behavior. However, if the parents choose to be uncooperative, you might be able to gain control of the situation by referring to a bullying situation that you did observe the same student do, but that the bullying victim did not report. Thus, the latest one must have been even worse for the student (victim) came to you to complain this time. Not only will this type of approach generally put you in control of the discussion, it may give you a little bit of a confidence boost and help you gain some more control of your emotions.

BUT THIS IS A
REALLY TOUGH CLASS

In any type of service occupation, we have to work in situations that may not be totally within our control. If we work at a store in the complaint department, we probably did not order the faulty merchandise. However, to the customers who ordered it, that is irrelevant. They do not have much concern about your perspective; they primarily care about what they want. The same thing is true with parents. For the most part, they only care about their child. And we are not saying this with any criticism. The parents who truly care about their children are often the least of our concerns. It is the parents who do not care about the children who create the most challenging situations.

With this in mind, we need to make sure that we accept responsibility for the situation and not try to pass the buck. It may be a challenging class, possibly your most challenging ever, but that does not matter to the parents. Their primary concern is how *their* child is doing.

If the most effective teacher in a school gives a test or homework assignment and the students do poorly on it—and this can happen to the best of us—who do they blame? Themselves. They feel that they should have explained it better or provided more guidance practice before they gave the independent assignment. And the real question is, who is the one person's behavior in that class they can control? Their own, of course.

If the least effective teacher in a school gives a test or homework assignment and the students do poorly on it, who do they blame? The students, last year's teacher, or maybe the parents.

The point of this is that trying to pass off responsibility to someone that we or the parents cannot control is a very temporary situation. It will only lead to greater frustration. In addition to shifting the responsibility away from us, it also shifts responsibility away from the parents and students. In actuality, that is where we want the responsibility focused.

Similar to complaining to a teacher or a principal about something in the school, the people who are sharing their concern with the complaint department do not care who is at fault, they just want the problem solved.

WHAT IF THEY TELL US NOT TO CALL THEM AT WORK?

Often the parents we have to deliver bad news to are the ones we have to contact on a very frequent basis. Sometimes we should give them a number on our speed dialing list. If we attempt to call these people at work, sometimes they will tell us that we cannot because they might get in trouble or even lose their jobs. For the average parent or an even mildly cooperative parent, I would work hard to comply. However, if I have a very disruptive student for which nothing seems to be working or tremendously uncooperative parents, I will make it a point to contact the parents at work. I will still always be nice and professional, however, if that is what it takes to get their attention or to motivate them to assist with the needs of their children, then I feel empowered and maybe even obligated to try every option that I have. It is important they become aware that the way to get me to stop calling them at work is for them to positively alter their child's behavior.

By the same token, if I am supposed to call Mom, and when I do, I hear from an angry Dad the next day, I will often switch and instead call Dad. Though he may be the most offensive party to work with, I might as well deal with him under my initiative rather than his. And hopefully I will also be down to just one phone call rather than two.

Despite our preparation and very best efforts, sometimes when we deliver less than positive news, the conversation can get heated. Being able to defuse the situation is critical. Several other chapters provide strategies and solutions for you, but we'd like to share one of our favorites now.

PLEASE DON'T TALK
TO ME LIKE THAT

We do believe it is important to allow people to let off a little steam. We all feel frustrated at times, and sometimes that is all it takes for someone to calm down. However, sometimes the tirade continues a little too long or becomes too ugly. What can we do? The single best method we have ever used we call "please don't talk to me like that." Again, like all communications, the style and approach we use will greatly determine its effectiveness. Let's take a look at the specific language involved.

If the parents have pushed my tolerance to the limit or they are being inappropriately personal or rude, here is I how respond. And keep in mind the tone I would use would be very calm, I would talk s-l-o-w and gentle, but I would want to have a quiet confidence in my voice. What I would say is:

> Mrs. Smith, please don't talk to me like that. I will *never* speak to you like that, and I will *never* speak to your son/daughter like that.

Realize that this is not a threat and it is not an order. Nobody likes to be told what to do, especially someone who is already angry. However, it does accomplish two things. It is a very reasonable and professional request, and it is a promise regarding how we will treat you and how we will treat your son or daughter. This is a very calming dialogue if we handle it in the correct manner. We try not to interrupt the other person at the beginning, but if it is past that point we might. However, the more heated the other party is, the slower and calmer we force ourselves to be. Another important thing about the above wording is that it is not inflammatory language. We did not want to ever incite an upset person.

Now realize that we also made a commitment ourselves regarding how we will treat that parents and their child. Of course, that should not be a problem because in order to deal with a difficult parent we first must be able to deal with ourselves!

When I was a principal I eventually had such confidence in the professionalism of my faculty and staff that I even added to it. As a principal with an incredibly dynamic staff, here is what I would say to calm a very, very upset parent who was being incredibly rude toward me:

> Mrs. Smith, please don't talk to me like that. I will *never* speak to you like that, and I will *never* speak to your son/daughter like that. And, no one in this school will ever speak to you like that, and no one in this school will ever speak to your son/daughter like that.

You can understand why I could only do this when I had a truly professional faculty. Because if even one person in the school would yell or speak in an unprofessional tone, then I had not kept my commitment, and then the parents really did have something to be upset about.

LITTLE PITCHERS HAVE BIG EARS

There is an old saying that "little pitchers have big ears." What this means is that as adults if we ever say anything we do not want children to repeat, then we had better make sure they do not hear us. This is critical in educator/parent communications. We will allow parents to vent for a while. However, we will not allow them to act inappropriately with the student present. We are happy to meet with them and discuss their issue, and we have no secrets to keep from their children. But we will not allow them to role-model improper behavior toward an educator in front of their child. Using the dialogue above is one way to help if you are meeting in person. And, obviously you can ask the child to step out of the office. However, if the parent calls you in the evening, you may not be as able to monitor who is present in the room.

And with our most challenging parents, often the student is there in the room with them egging them on. We do believe it is essential to attempt to prevent this from occurring. If we feel that the child is listening to inappropriate behavior on the part of the parent, we will say to the parent:

I sure hope that there is no chance that Gregory can hear this conversation. I would be very disappointed if he could hear you talking to anyone in our school in this manner. I would never want him to get the impression that we can ever talk to someone in our school in that tone of voice, so I sure hope that is no chance Gregory can hear you speaking to me this way.

We are sure that this did not always work, but we feel that it was doing two things. One is just trying to help the parents understand that their son being privy to this conversation was wrong. And the other is that this is another method that can help the parents get control of themselves and stop their inappropriate behavior.

SUMMING UP

There are many different approaches to delivering bad news to a parent. The first step is to decide what you want to say and how you want to say it. Another important facet is to develop as many resources and tools that can help you if the parent chooses not to respond in as appropriate a manner as you may wish. Also, keep in mind that as you develop your skills, sometimes we have to go into what is called the broken record mode and keep revisiting key points. Maybe four or five times in the conversation we have to refocus on the future by continuing to come back to, "Okay, Mrs. Smith, now what can we do to make sure that this behavior does not occur again?" Maintaining the proper focus can allow you to be in more control of yourself and as a result be in more control of the situation.

Always remember, also, that sometimes the parents who are most belligerent in defending their child are doing it out of guilt. They may be well aware that they have not been as attentive to the needs of their child as they should have been, so yelling at you is one way to show they care. And, unfortunately for some of our most challenging parents, it may be the only way they have shown that they care.

12

But I Did Get a Good Deal— Examining the Car Salesman

One experience that most of us has had is buying a car from a car dealership. Though we may cringe at the possibility of having to haggle when we go in, most people feel when they leave that they got a "good deal." To emphasize this point, I often present groups with the following scenario.

How many of you have bought a car from a car dealer over the last three years? In a group of 100 people, usually 80+ percent of the hands go up. Then I ask, "How many of you think you got a good deal?" Almost as may hands go up. I then say, "Okay, now those of you who have not bought cars from dealers in the last three years, how many of you think that those people who raised their hands *really* got a good deal?" Amazingly no hands go up. I then say, okay, those of you who have purchased a car, how many of you *really* think you got a good deal? How many of you think you really snookered that dealership? Interestingly, very few people logically think they got a good deal, but emotionally many of us do. Even after going through this process, some people are still upset emotionally.

That shows the power of the car dealer. Even though logically we never get a "good deal," emotionally we feel that we do. Understanding this dynamic can be very beneficial in effectively interacting with parents, and anyone else for that matter. Several things happen. One of the most obvious when we look at it objectively, but potentially the most effective, is that the salesman makes you *feel* that he or she is on your side. The other item to understand is that potentially in your mind you are comparing the original or sticker price of the car to the final price that you actually paid. And, since generally there is a fairly significant difference, you again feel that you got a good deal.

Or the other concept dealing with price is that the price you received when you traded in your car was more than you were hoping to get, thus again leaving you feeling like you received a good deal on the car. Now, objectively we know that the sticker price was not really the price, and we are also aware that the price they gave us for our trade was actually just a discount off of the list price of the car we purchased, nonetheless, it makes us feel much more satisfied with the final outcome. My purpose in sharing this is not to have us debate whether or not you are a master negotiator, the point is to help you understand what effective negotiators do. And, what is even more ironic is that the more you want to argue that you did get a good deal, the more it probably proves the point that the dealer was successful in making you feel satisfied.

I want to share one more example to show the point of the deal maker. For several years when I worked in a particular school district, I had the pleasure of transporting our opening session speakers to and from the airport. One year I had a well-known gentlemen who had formerly been involved in professional sports. He did a nice job as a speaker, and I was taking him back to the airport. Making conversation, I asked him what he did now that he was out of sports. He said that he did negotiation seminars around the country. I commented that that must be very interesting. I then brought up my theory regarding car dealers. I asked him why he thought it was that everyone who buys a car thinks they got a good deal, and yet no one really gets a good deal. He laughed and agreed. Then he got very serious and sort of defiantly said, "You know in general that is true, but last month I bought a new car and I *did* get a good deal!"

That shows the emotional power of the car deal. A person who does negotiations for a living still is insistent that he got a good deal. Wow!

With that in mind, I always set out to make sure that people felt that they were treated fairly and with respect. However, in the toughest situations or in working with the most difficult people, I set an even higher standard. I actually wanted people to thank me when we were done visiting. As an assistant principal and principal, my goal was to have parents thank me when I suspended their son or daughter. That may sound like a lofty goal, but it is one that I feel that we can reach at least 90 percent of the time. Keep in mind that there is no more potentially adversarial relationship than working with car dealers. Trust me, they have the exact opposite interest than you have. Their goal is to make you spend as much money as possible, and your goal is to spend as little. If car dealers can make you feel like you got a good deal when they definitely do not have your best interests in mind, then educators can accomplish this same goal. At least in education, both the parents and school personnel have the same interest in mind—doing what is best for the student. Let's take a look at how this concept can work.

LET ME TAKE ANOTHER LOOK
UNDERNEATH THAT HOOD

If as a teacher you walk into a smoky student restroom in your school and there are two nervous students in there, it would be nice if you could approach them in a way in which they would admit they were smoking. If they denied they were doing anything wrong then it would be very tough to resolve the situation. You did not really see them smoke, and even if you did, they might still choose to deny it. How could we best get them to come clean?

What we have found to be effective is to ask the students, "Do you all smoke in here every day or is this your first time?" Even sophisticated students are likely to respond, "It's our first time." You then treat them as if it is the first time they have smoked, they get suspended or whatever the consequences are, and you make sure their parents are aware that they admitted it. You even tell the students, "Since this is your first time and you admitted it, we'll only go with a three-day suspension." Even though the first occurrence always results in a three-day suspension, the students and parents are much more likely to be appreciative that they "got a good deal."

As a principal, I found this same approach to be effective with challenging parents. I remember once that I had a new assistant principal and a parent came into the office complaining very loudly that their child had been treated unfairly. This parent was offensive, rude, and overbearing. Quite a pleasant trifecta. Anyhow, I went out in the main office area and asked the parent if I could help him. The parent went on to complain that his child had been suspended by the assistant principal, Mr. Johnson, for three days, and that was not fair. I invited this parent into my office, and he bellowed on about how unfair a three-day suspension was for his son.

I lowered my voice and talked in the slowest and quietest tone I could and asked the parent to tell me what happened. He described what his son had been accused of doing and continually refocused on the fact that the punishment his son received (the three-day suspension) from the assistant principal was unfair. Finally, again in the calmest voice I could muster, I said to the parent, "I had not heard about this situation until just now, but it does sound unfair." The parent relaxed and started to get a smug look on his face. I then continued.

"I'll have to look into this, but it sounds to me like Mr. Johnson did not handle this correctly." The parent continued to get a very satisfied expression. I then added very nicely, but firmly, "No, this doesn't sound fair. It sounds like your son should have been suspended for five days. As a matter of fact, I can make sure, because you seemed so unhappy with him, that Mr. Johnson doesn't deal with your son in the future." Then, before the parent could interrupt, I continued with, "If you would like, I will look into this tomorrow, and I will not allow Mr. Johnson to be involved. It sounds like he was really trying to work with you and your son by only giving him a three-day out. However, as I said, if you would like me to, I'll visit with the people involved tomorrow and I'll call you with the results. Since your son is already going to be home, I can just call you and add on the additional days. If you would like, I'll check into it first thing and give you a call as soon as I find out anything."

The parent immediately jumped up and said, "Well, you know, now that I think about it, I think that Mr. Johnson was okay after all. My son said he thought that Mr. Johnson was trying to be helpful, so I won't take up any more of your time. I think that Mr. Johnson was just doing his job, and I am sorry that I bothered you. Thanks for your help, but just forget that I ever came in. Have a good day."

It was amazing—this very belligerent parent went from insisting that this assistant principal was horribly unfair to thanking me and saying that he thought Mr. Johnson was bending over backwards to help his son. I guess maybe he thought that he got a "good deal" after all. Interestingly, this parent, who had a terrible reputation, never came in to complain again.

Now, I realize that this is not always appropriate, and it should be used sparingly. However, when dealing with the most challenging of parents, I always liked to keep it on reserve. But gentler versions of this same approach can be very beneficial and used more frequently.

As a teacher, being able to say things like, "because she told the truth..." or "since it is the first week of school..." can be regular approaches that help people feel that they were got off lighter than they might have otherwise.

Principals can use language like, "normally this would be a 10-day suspension, but because . . ." or "we have had students removed from the team for the entire season for things like this but since you have been so supportive..." This approach can also be helpful to reinforce positive behaviors and approaches on the part of parents as well as students.

Though a person may spend $4.00 on gas to drive to another store to save $2.50, they still *feel* like it was a bargain. Keeping this in mind can help you approach parents in a way that will make them feel more supported.

Oftentimes as educators, we reduce negative consequences in our own mind before we share them with students or parents. We are a caring profession with sensitive people. In general, that is a positive. However, at times, being a little more manipulative may be of benefit.

Let's look at a fairly common situation of a student cheating on a quiz. We can react angrily and mentally decide that this student will flunk the quiz and be assigned three hours detention. However, before we share that with the student and parent we think to ourselves that she is generally a nice young lady, and it hasn't happened before, so we decide to tell the student that she will flunk the quiz and have to stay after school an hour. Then you call the parents that evening, or, before you have the opportunity, they call you angry that their daughter is being "double punished." First the F and then staying after school.

Then, you try to defend yourself by angrily saying, "I should have given her three hours detention!" Next thing you know, you are in an argument, and you are really ticked off because in your mind you had already given the girl a break. Whatever the resolution to the situation finally is, both parties are upset. Even if you do not change your mind, you feel as though you gave in too much, and they are upset that you did not give in enough.

However, the approach could have been to tell the girl that she will receive an F on the quiz, and you are considering giving her three to five hours detention—you want to think about it for awhile. Then, that evening after she has communicated with her parents the potential consequences, you call the parents and tell them how serious the situation is, but that you are also aware that she has not been in trouble before, so you are willing to adjust her punishment to an F and an hour detention. It is amazing how effective it is when you mention a more severe consequence, even fleetingly. The reduced punishment sounds so much better to the student and the parents.

I remember once that I wanted to get two cats. My wife was not too crazy about having a house pet of any kind. However, finally I got the nerve to ask if we could get three cats. She responded, "Three cats! No way can we get more than two cats." I hope she doesn't read this part of the book because until now she thinks she has gotten a pretty good deal.

GOOD FOR 90 DAYS
OR 3,000 MILES

Obviously this approach is not applicable in every situation, and we have to use it judiciously in order for it to be effective. If every time you tried to buy cereal in a store you had to dicker for the actual price this would get very old and annoying. Yet, doing it once in a while for a major purchase makes us feel special. Repeatedly or always taking this same approach will have diminishing or even negative returns.

However, remembering the basic concept of making people feel like they were treated fairly, or maybe even that they got a good deal, can go a long way in developing and maintaining positive relations. This is the type of approach that we can put in our bag of tricks and pull out when we have an especially challenging parent or an especially difficult situation. Understanding the concept and being aware of how it can apply to many situations can allow us to build a reserve of approaches that we can use during the most challenging times.

APPLYING IT TO THE CLASSROOM

A scenario that all classroom teachers dread, but many of us have faced, is when irate or obnoxious parents show up at your door and demand their child leave with them right now. Not only can this be intimidating to us, but it is horribly embarrassing for the student. Additionally, if they have not gone through the office, you may not even know if they are legally a parent or guardian of the child. How do we handle this? Let's think of our automobile hawking friend.

The real power of the car salesman is that they make the customers feel that they are on their side. Though they at worst really represent the car dealership, and at best, themselves, effective salespeople have the ability to make you feel that they are representing you.

Understand that many belligerent parents feel very resentful toward authority. They may not get along with their boss, they may have trouble with the law, and they may resent school people because of their past experiences. However, working to get on their side can be very beneficial.

My first year as a teacher I was in a rural setting. One day when I was teaching, a man who appeared very intoxicated walked in the doorway of my class and loudly slurred, "I'm here to pick up Johnny. Let's go boy—now!" I was pretty confident he had not checked in at the office for a pass. I also had no idea what his relationship was with the student, and the alcohol smell he was emitting was an additional concern. The only thing I could think of was getting him away from the students and down to the office. Because my classroom did not have an intercom to call the office, I had few choices. And, to be honest, if I am really concerned about a parent's stability, I would rather not dive for the intercom switch and raise his level of concern if I can help in anyhow. So, mentally I put on my white shoes and slid into the sales mode.

I walked calmly toward the man and introduced myself. After very gingerly asking him if he had stopped by the office and getting brashly rebuked, I then shifted modes. I matched his demeanor and explained, "I am sorry to tell you, but you know the world nowadays. Nobody trusts honest people like you and me. We're always getting jacked around. Anyhow, because of that, good guys like us are always gettin' hassled. So now, they make us go down to the office and check in. It sounds silly, but that's the deal we all have to fight. It would sure help me out if we could go down there. I'll show you where it is."

It was like this guy and I became best friends. We had the "world's against us" bond. He started saying things like, "damn right" and "good guys like us," but next thing you know we were heading down to the office. I caught another teacher's eye to watch my class, and we walked down to the office together just complaining about how the "world's fallin' apart." Another 10 minutes, and I could have sold him my late model Ford that had only been driven on Sundays.

NEGOTIATING ZERO TOLERANCE

One limiting situation that may seem to be common today is the use of "zero tolerance" policies in many schools. That is a situation where there is a prescribed punishment required for a specific offense. Oftentimes it is most common when there are weapons or drugs involved. However, some of the techniques we have just described can still be applied. Keep in mind the importance of working to make parents feel that we are on their side. Let's see how this can apply to a zero tolerance situation.

If your school has a policy of a one semester expulsion for drugs, then you can still work to get on the side of parents. How? By showing concern for the student's success even in this situation. First off, you can always rely on using the technique in Chapter 9 of expressing your sorrow by sharing that, "I am truly sorry that this happened." Though you may not even be sorry this student is being dismissed from the school, you are still sorry it happened, or else you could put your time and energy into something more pleasant and productive.

Another point is to "focus on the future." This is described at length in Chapter 14, but the idea is to shift to what it is we can do now. In other words, show genuine concern for the students' continuing their education during the time they are out of your school. Suggest some other school settings that may accept them—either private or alternative public settings. Even if there is little chance that these schools will accept them (and of course, you would not share the unlikelihood of this), the parents and students might still appreciate your concern and ideas. There is no reason to leave anyone with a sour taste in their mouth. Though it might be a challenge, showing personal concern and interest can soften their ire.

Also, there is a very selfish interest in this. If students are removed from your school but may eventually return, you want to do everything you can to keep them on track to move up grade levels. Though you might wonder why, keep in mind that if you do not, when they return they will just be in your school that much longer! Like the car salesman, there is definitely some advantage in working to be on their side.

13

WHAT IF THEY USE THE "F" WORD— FAIR?

One challenge that every educator faces is when there is an accusation that something is not fair. Every teacher has a "classroom lawyer" who is constantly in the "It's not fair!" mode in life. As experienced teachers, though, this may still become exasperating. We have often developed ways to reduce the amount of "fair debates" that occur in our classrooms. We may have established an effective approach that works with students; however, it is essential that we can also work with parents when they accuse us of not being fair with their child.

Though it is not an appropriate response in the classroom, a teacher may even say something sarcastic like, "Well, life is not fair," or "This isn't a democracy!" As undesirable as this type of response is, it may at least work temporarily in the classroom with people much younger than us or with an imbalance of power, though it will probably eventually escalate into a more negative confrontation.

It reminds me of an old joke. A teacher sarcastically says to a student, "What do you think?" The student then snaps back, "Well, what do *you* think?" The teacher smugly drawls, "Well, I don't think . . . I know!" And the student quips a reply of, "Well, I don't think I know either!"

This type of interchange is unprofessional with students, and it is totally unacceptable with parents. With that in mind, how can we best respond to the parent who pulls out the "F" word on us—fair?

BE FAIR, BE SQUARE, OR
BE BOTH LIKE ME

Obviously, one of the first things that we need to do in order to diminish the amount of "that's not fair" comments is to be fair. Not only, of course, to be fair, but to be perceived as being fair. Gary Phillips (1997) once said that, "Treating unequals equally is no justice." We do agree. If we are working with people, especially young people, there are always going to be situations in which we cannot have a predetermined response. There are always going to be judgment calls. However, any time that we can have predetermined expectations and consequences that we have communicated appropriately can help to reduce the unfair chanting. Of course, even these predetermined standards must be reasonable.

We described a situation in Chapter 12 in which one of the authors gave a zero to students who did not have their homework assignment with them at the beginning of class. If they left it in the locker, tough luck. As you may recall, this went fine for most of the first semester. Only a few students forgot their work, and they were primarily the lower-achieving students anyhow. Additionally, most of the assignments were routine homework that would not dramatically affect their grade to any significant degree.

Then, close to the end of the semester, one of the best and most responsible students in the class forgot a major assignment. It was left in her locker, which was just outside the classroom. It would significantly impact her grade for not only the quarter, but the entire first semester. As was described in Chapter 12, I knew I was wrong and that ended my rule. And, the only thing that I could do to be fair was let any of the students who had fallen prey to this ill-thought rule turn in their missing assignments. However, realizing this error before the parent got involved went a long way in avoiding a "you're not fair" battle that I could not feel good about.

THREE RESPONSES
TO THE FAIR WORD

We'd like to share three things that have been effective in dealing with parents (or others) when they assert that you have not been fair. Interestingly enough, all three of them require you using the F(air) word yourself regularly in response. We will talk about a situation as a teacher, one as a coach, and one as a principal defending someone else's actions. All three approaches can be utilized regardless of our position or responsibilities.

THE IT-WOULDN'T-BE-FAIR-IF-I-DIDN'T Approach

Let's say that I did attempt to defend my behavior regarding the zero for any homework assignment. If I received a call from the parent of that particular student that night—we'll call the student Ricky and the parent Mr. Ricardo—in which the parent brought up the lack of fairness in the way his son was affected, here is how I would respond.

> I appreciate your concern about fair. And what wouldn't be fair, Mr. Ricardo, is if I *didn't* do that. You sound like you are very concerned about *fair* and so am I. And I would not want your son treated unfairly, so in order to treat him *fairly*, I have no other choice. I know that you want Ricky treated the same as the other 120 students I have in my classes so that everything is *fair*. And if I didn't give him a zero, it wouldn't be *fair*, so I appreciate your regard for treating your son in the same manner as the other students. So, the only way I can be *fair* is to give him a zero. And I value very much your understanding of the importance of being *fair*.

Now, with all approaches in which the educator is the aggressor, there is a fine line between being confident and assertive and smart alec and sarcastic. However, having a calm tone and a predetermined dialogue can go a long way toward diminishing the lack of fairness approach. Interestingly, we recommend that the more the parents are hung up on this "fair" issue, the more we would use the word fair in our response. If they are very nice and cooperative, we may not even use the word in our reply. However, if they are aggressive parents who center their life on not being treated fairly, then we would sprinkle "fair" very liberally into our response. Again, of course, we must always remain calm and work hard to maintain a very confident tone.

As a principal, I would use this same approach. If a student was being suspended for a fight in the cafeteria, and the parents felt like his punishment was unfair, I would apply the following dialogue.

> I appreciate your concern about being fair, because you and I have the same point of view that is it essential that all students, including your son, be treated fairly. It is essential that everyone in the school be treated fairly. And I know that you want your son to be treated the same as the other students in the school. So it is critical that he be treated the same as the 250 students in the cafeteria would be if they had been the ones involved in a fight. Since every student in the school has received the same punishment for fighting during the three years that I have been principal here, the only fair thing to do is to treat him exactly the same as every other student in the school. And, I would not want your son to be accused of not being treated fairly because of me not suspending him. And I sure would not want the other parents to think you weren't being treated fairly, or the other 250 students that saw him fight ever accuse him of being favored or of not being treated in a fair manner. Thus, the only choice I have in order to be fair is to suspend your son. And I appreciate greatly your regard for every student in this school, including your son, being treated fairly.

Again, the manner and tone we use is essential. Maintaining a confident and professional voice and disposition is critical. As soon as any hint of sarcasm enters your voice, you have just triggered an escalation of this situation, so it is very important that you maintain and monitor the way you deliver your response.

MY DAUGHTER'S NOT GETTING ENOUGH PLAYING TIME—IT'S NOT FAIR

A situation that every coach has to deal with at some time is a parent saying that their son or daughter is not playing enough on the team. This occurs at every level of sports. Keeping in the mind the previous approach, that it wouldn't be fair if I didn't, is the idea that it wouldn't be fair if I did. Here is an example.

If you are a coach of a basketball team and a parent approaches you after practice one day and says, "It's not fair— you do not play my daughter in the varsity games enough!" A potential response that is very effective is to say the following:

> Right now your daughter is the ninth best player on the team and the fourth best guard. I am playing her about 5 minutes a game based on her being the ninth best player and the fourth best guard. As you probably know, typically I play our third best guard about 14 minutes a game. However, if your daughter continues to work and practice hard, she may at some point in the future be the third best, second best, or even possibly the best guard on the team. What would not be fair is if at that point she did not get to play as much as the top guards do right now. And, I would expect you to be upset with me if she becomes the third best guard on the team and she doesn't get to play about 14 minutes a game. However, it would not be fair if I did play her more now as fourth best guard because that would limit the time she might receive in the future if she continues to improve.

It is important to help parents and others to understand how being fair now can benefit their son or daughter as their son's or daughter's circumstances change. It also allows the parent and student to focus on something—working to improve the student's skills.

YOU'RE RIGHT, IT ISN'T FAIR— IT SHOULD BE A FIVE-DAY SUSPENSION

The example given in Chapter 12 regarding the parent accusing an assistant principal of not being fair when he suspended a student for three days is a classic example of this approach. As principal, I was able to respond, "that doesn't seem fair, it doesn't seem fair at all. Why don't you let me look into that? Typically that is a five-day suspension. If what you are telling me is correct, it sounds like Mr. Johnson (the assistant principal) made a mistake. I'll tell you what, I won't let him deal with this situation. Instead, I'll deal with it. Go ahead and keep your son home for the three days and I'll call you tomorrow with the additional days after I look into it. It sure doesn't sound like Mr. Johnson was fair."

It is amazing that if you approach this correctively, the parent will think that hindsight being 20-20, that Mr. Johnson was very fair. As a matter of fact, if they really thought about it, he may be the most fair person they have ever known!

APPROACH IS EVERYTHING

Seriously, again the approach you take is essential. Being calm, relaxed, confident, and assertive all at the same time is needed. Practicing the specific words in the dialogue can allow you to be able to pull them out of your tool kit at the most opportune times. Again, you'll notice in all three situations that the more the parents are hung up on the "fair" word, the more it will be in my response. If they are going to try to use it as a weapon, then I am going to pull the "F" word out of my holster in reply. However, you can pair that up with a confident and professional tone that will allow you to make your point in an effective manner.

14

FOCUS ON THE FUTURE

Many times when dealing with challenging parents we have issues that are difficult to reach agreement on. The version that their child gives could possibly vary "slightly" from the one that we have. Also, they may not agree with the consequence that occurs because of their son's or daughter's action. However, finding some common ground that we can agree on is essential. It would be especially valuable if we even have a perspective or point of view that the student, parent, and teacher can all agree on. We can have that perspective by focusing on the future.

FOCUS ON THE FUTURE

When handling discipline as an assistant junior high principal, I found that often parents did not agree with the consequences that their child received or sometimes even disagreed with any punishment at all. Working with these people to develop a common ground and understanding was very critical to being successful and feeling supported as a school. Additionally, the students may not feel that any punishments they have received are just. However, I did learn that all parties involved can agree on one thing. And that is that they did not want it to happen again. Shifting the focus from the present—which we might not all agree about—to the future can allow for the development of this common understanding. I'll share with you an example about administering discipline regarding the school bus.

THE DRIVER ON THE BUS
SAID, "MOVE ON BACK..."

A popular children's song has a verse that goes, "The driver on the bus said, "Move on back, move on back, move on back."'" However, nowhere in the song does a student say, "Why don't you try and make me!" Thus, we know the driver was not the driver of a school bus. As assistant principal, one of my responsibilities was to handle the bus reports that drivers sent forward for approximately 600 eighth grade students who rode the bus each day. Well, as you can imagine, this was quite a challenge. In addition to the potentially varying skills of the 30+ drivers, seldom did any of them actually observe the entire sequence of events that occurred which resulted in the students receiving a disciplinary bus "ticket." If we think managing a classroom is a challenge, just imagine trying to manage two entire classrooms while driving! Anyhow, what often resulted were bus reports that were potentially debatable.

The policy of the school district was that the first bus ticket was a warning, the second bus ticket was 5 days off the bus, the next ticket was 10 days off the bus, the next ticket was 20 days off the bus, and so on. The same consequence was to occur whether the student threw a paper wad, was out of his/her seat, or used obscene language to the bus driver. Not exactly the best policy to attempt to enforce.

One of the things that I quickly realized about these situations was that ever determining exactly what happened would be difficult at best. Additionally, many times multiple students were involved, but the driver only reported one or a few of the guilty parties. Sorting this all out was next to impossible. However, I did learn that focusing on the future was a critical element in attempting to resolve the challenge of getting parents to be supportive. Let's look at a specific situation.

When I received a bus ticket, it listed the student's name, the offense, and the bus number. Typically, the amount of detail on the offense would be something to the effect of one of these terms: cussing, out of seat, yelling, rowdy, disruptive, and the like. Usually these tickets would arrive two to three days after the incident occurred, and the driver's ability to recall details were shaky, to put it kindly.

I would call the student down to the office and share that I received a bus report, and ask him or her to tell me what occurred. Sometimes the student would admit to something, but many times it was a different interpretation than the driver may have presented in the two- or three-word report. All of us have the skills to work effectively with students to at least get them to admit some possible wrongdoing. However, the real challenge was in contacting the parents. Here is how the conversation allowed for a focusing on the future.

> "Hi, Mrs. Johnson. This is Bill Smith, assistant principal at Eastside Junior High. I am sorry to bother you at work but I wanted you to know that I received a bus report on Matthew for being out of his seat yesterday on the school bus. This is Matthew's first bus report, which is a warning. However, if Matthew receives a bus report in the future then it will result in a five-day suspension from the school bus."

Realize that what I did was get away from the details of this situation (which I seldom knew much about anyhow) to shifting to the future. We would then have the typical discussion asking if Matthew had shared this information with them, and I would let them know that he was sitting right here if they would like to visit with him. Then I would once again look to the future to conclude the conversation.

> "Mrs. Johnson I would appreciate you visiting with Matthew tonight regarding the importance of proper behavior on the school bus, because as we had mentioned, if he receives a bus report in the future it will result in a five-day bus suspension, and none of us want that to occur."

A couple of things happened with this approach. We moved from something I didn't really know much about—his bus behavior—to something that we all agree on—that we did not want it to happen again. Additionally, if you think back to

Chapter 12, on examining the car salesman, the two things the parents remember are that this ticket is a warning and that the next one is a five-day suspension. And, when parents hear the two terms, they realize that the warning sounds like a pretty good deal after all. Additionally, if you do happen to get another call from them, the parents already know the consequence. In the future, if there is another bus report here is how the conversation goes.

> "Hi, Mrs. Johnson. This is Bill Smith, assistant principal at Eastside Junior High. I am sorry to bother you at work, but I wanted you to know that I received a bus report on Matthew for throwing paper yesterday on the school bus."

It is amazing how many times at this point the parent would interrupt and say, "I know, I know, five days off the bus."

Regardless of their response, though, I would at some point reconvene the dialogue with, "As you might be aware, this is Matthew's second bus report, and the second report is a five-day suspension from the bus. However, if Matthew receives a bus report in the future, then it will result in a 10-day suspension from the school bus."

Then at some point I would conclude the conversation with, "Mrs. Johnson, I would appreciate you visiting with Matthew tonight regarding the importance of proper behavior on the school bus, because as we had mentioned, if he receives a bus report in the future it will result in a 10-day bus suspension and none of us wants that to occur."

And, none of us did want that occur. Additionally, getting a five-day suspension did not sound as bad as what would happen next. Also, it made the future call easier if one was going to have to be made.

This exact approach is just as applicable from the standpoint of the classroom teacher. Whether we initiate a parental contact or we receive an unexpected one, being ready to shift to the future can be very beneficial. In the next section, we describe another example of specific language that may help us alter the focus from the present to the future.

WHAT CAN WE DO TO MAKE SURE THAT THIS DOESN'T HAPPEN AGAIN?

Another way to make the shift to the future is to ask, "What can we do to make sure this doesn't happen again?" Again, we bring a point forward that we can both concur on—that neither of us wants it to happen again. Making sure that we listen, remain calm, and show a genuine interest in a parent's concerns are essential in order to develop credibility and build positive relations. However, it is just as critical that we have specific dialogue that we can rely on in order to help guide difficult conversations to an appropriate and productive conclusion.

The same concept, described in Chapter 13, regarding focusing on the future occurred when we called parents and asked for their help. If a child does not have supplies, asking the parents for their help in the future is an effective way to move the conversation from the present to the future. And, one thing we know about effective student behavior management is that effective people are always looking to prevent misbehavior from occurring again, and less effective behavior managers are looking for revenge for past misbehavior. The basic and most important reason that it is more productive to look to the future is that there is not anything we can do about the behavior that has already occurred. The only thing we can do is to attempt to prevent it from happening again.

PRACTICE MAKES PERFECT (OR AT LEAST IT MAKES BETTER)

Getting all sides to realize the benefit to looking forward to something we can influence is much more empowering then only centering on things that we cannot control. Developing the skills to effectively guide the conversation to the future can be very beneficial. Realize that this skill is appropriate in almost every situation, so we have the opportunity to try it out in more comfortable settings where we are prepared and familiar with the specific language and dialogue. This will allow us to tap into our mental tape recorder and smoothly pull out our focus on the future language during the more stressful and trying settings we may encounter.

PART V

INCREASING PARENTAL INVOLVEMENT

15

UNDERSTANDING PARENT INVOLVEMENT

Getting and keeping parents involved in our schools is a necessary first step toward developing understanding. The more parents are involved in our schools, the more they understand the struggles and challenges that face educators today. An obvious by-product of this understanding is that these parents become much easier to deal with. They realize that we are all caring, committed educators who want what is best for their children. Even when they question decisions that we may make, they do so in a much more agreeable manner. As an example, consider the comments made by local business or community members after they have visited your school. If you have had the pleasure of involving these individuals in school activities, you have probably heard them make statements such as, "Wow, I never realized just how hard teachers work."

Involving parents at home, as will be elaborated on in Chapter 17, pays similar dividends. When parents are aware of school activities, involved in school governance in some capacity, or helping with their child's homework, then they have a greater understanding of what takes place at school on a regular basis. Consequently, they become much more understanding and easier to deal with. The important techniques described in previous chapters of this book will not need to be used as often if we are able to make parents less difficult by getting and keeping them involved.

As is mentioned in Chapter 2, parent involvement is unquestionably one of the most significant factors influencing student achievement. Throughout the past decade, there have been numerous reports and a large body of research stating that parent involvement is a critical factor in the success of students (Benson, Buckley, and Elliott, 1980; Epstein, 1992; Rioux and Berla, 1993). In fact, to back this research up, an eighth goal dealing with parental participation was recently added to the now famous National Education Goals (Goals 2000). Specifically, the eighth goal is stated as: "Every school will promote partnerships that will increase parental involvement and participation in promoting the social, emotional, and academic growth of children." (Achieving the Goals, 1997). The wording of this goal, after careful analysis, acknowledges parental involvement's ability to promote social, emotional, and academic growth. There are many school mission statements, vision statements, and statements of belief throughout this country that mention the school's role in promoting student growth in all three of these areas. If parental involvement really is a key to our success in this regard, then is it not time to pay serious attention to it?

The addition of the eighth goal therefore illustrates, in large part, the federal government's acknowledgment of parents' significance in education. This significance had not previously been acknowledged so strongly by any federal agency. Recognizing this significance, the National Parent Teacher Association (PTA) devised a list of six national standards with the sole purpose of promoting meaningful parent and family participation in 1997. This organization has also led to many studies during recent years with the purpose of exploring the nature and intent of parents' involvement in their children's education. The rest of us have finally begun to recognize its merits.

The cries for parental involvement and the understanding of its impact on student success are coming from the ranks of both elementary and secondary schools. In a 1996 report of the National Association of Secondary School Principals entitled *Breaking Ranks*, a strong recommendation was made that high schools actively engage students' families as educational partners. Additionally, the National Association of Elementary School Principals has a Web site dedicated to the role parent involvement plays in student achievement (http://www. naesp.org/students/sslinks.htm). This site links to various other locations touting the benefits of parental involvement in schools. Among the linked sites are those sponsored by the U.S. Department of Education and the National PTA.

In further recognition of the benefits of parental involvement in education, some large urban school districts have dramatically increased their focus on this variable in very recent years. The Chicago Public Schools, for example, are beginning to provide parents with reports that will focus on the parents' own role in their children's education. These reports, in the form of checklists, are designed to ascertain the extent to which parents are supporting the school's efforts at home, as well as the parent's success at discharging their own parental duties. Items evaluated include academic ones, such as whether or not students are completing homework assignments and arriving at school with the necessary materials, and parental ones, such as whether or not students are eating breakfast in the morning and arriving at school with the proper medication and clothing appropriate for the weather.

Paul G. Vallas, the Chief Executive Officer of Chicago's 430,000-student school district believes that this new plan will reach out to parents by evaluating their involvement. He says, "The bottom line is: We are either going to talk the talk or walk the walk. Let's stop complaining about parent involvement and do something about it" (Galley, 2000).

While attention has been increasingly focusing on the benefits of parental involvement in schools, the notion of this participation is hardly contemporary. To the contrary, parental involvement in our public schools, both when it was strongly present and noticeably absent, has been a major factor in determining everything from scheduling to curricular choices since before the birth of our country. To understand this and relate it to present parent involvement dilemmas, think about some of the changes parental roles in schooling have undergone. Whereas at one time parents were absent or only in supporting roles relative to their children's schooling, many of them now take on much more decisive roles. Consider the summary in the following section as a description of the transitions parental roles have undergone in schooling.

PARENTS OF THE PAST

Many years ago, near the time of our nation's birth, parents had total control over their children's schooling. Since compulsory attendance laws did not exist, parents had complete authority in deciding how much schooling, if any, their children were to receive. Likewise, because there was far less variety in religious and cultural beliefs than we experience in America today, parents were virtually assured that their values and beliefs would be advanced in school. Additionally, the lack of depth and breadth in curricular choices almost created a guarantee to parents that they would be cognizant of what their children learned in school. Parent involvement primarily consisted of reinforcing skills and values that were taught in the schoolhouse. However, the desires of parents with regard to the quantity and quality of schooling their children would receive figured prominently into schoolhouse decisions.

As times progressed, parents saw their roles and the degree of their involvement change a bit. Over time, a new mission for education emerged. Where schools had previously advanced the morals and ethos of families, it quickly became important that they advanced and protected our American culture as well. Parents, though very supportive of the school's goals in creating an educated citizenry, were slowly becoming less involved in the actual structures and designs of these institutions. In their place, now famous educators like Noah Webster were making decisions regarding what should be taught and how instruction should be delivered. In advancing his belief that the United States should have a uniquely American language, Webster, along with William Holmes McGuffy, strongly influenced curriculum during this period. Instead of merely reading the Bible, readers such as the famous *McGuffy Reader* became the norm. Parents, valuing the patriotism, heroism, and strong work ethic schools professed, were highly supportive of American school's endeavors and continued to reinforce their teachings at home. The major curricular decisions, however, were still left to the experts.

As our nation became more global and industrialized, educational theories from other parts of the world quickly infiltrated our American beliefs. The kindergarten movement, born in Germany, is but one example. Additionally, the government became increasingly involved in decisions regarding our schools. Many parents, lacking a strong educational background themselves, began yielding more to the authority of experts regarding what schools should teach and how they should teach it. This is not to say that parents simply gave up all interest in their children's education. To the contrary, many were very involved and supportive. Their involvement had changed, however. Rather than being influential in deciding the content of school curricula, parents were now more involved in supporting the school's decisions. This support manifested itself in fundraising efforts like bake sales and in organized groups, such as PTAs and PTOs. Mothers became the primary supporters of schools while fathers, making up most of the American workforce, took a backseat role.

The preceding paragraphs by no means characterize all aspects of parental roles in American education during a 200-year period. Nor do they acknowledge the differences that existed within and between various American communities. Instead, they merely generalize the role parents played to allow us to better understand the differences between these behaviors and the behaviors of parents today.

CONTEMPORARY PARENT INVOLVEMENT

During the second half of the 1900s and continuing today, the role of parents in relation to their children's schools has undergone significant transitions. These transitions have tended to mirror the transitions that have taken place within the larger society. Most notably changed has been the family structure itself. As discussed in Chapter 1, these societal changes have dramatically altered the appearance of the American workforce, thus seriously limiting the time many parents have to be involved in their children's education. Consider these two points: The proportion of married women with children who were working outside the home rose from 41 percent in 1975 to 63 percent in 1999; In 1999, 23 percent of children lived in single-parent families (U.S. Bureau of the Census, 1999). There is good reason to believe that both of these figures are on the rise. Ignoring the fact that schools must change how and when we reach out to parents from these homes is to ignore the very nature of these changes.

As mentioned earlier, of equal significance is the fact that many parents of today had very negative experiences in school when they were children. This is truer today than it was when curricular choices were limited, compulsory attendance laws were absent or unenforced, and the requirements put on education by the American workforce were lighter burdens to bear. In a 1992 survey conducted by The National PTA (www. ncpie.org), 25 percent of parents reported that they feel intimidated by their children's schools. If 25 percent admitted these feelings of intimidation, isn't it possible that others may have been feeling them as well? I know that if my time is limited and I must choose between participating in an activity I enjoy or participating in an activity that intimidates me, my choice becomes rather simple. These things must all be considered in examining parent attitudes and involvement in our schools today.

After consideration of these points, it is significant to point out some elements of what good parental involvement looks like at the dawn of this new century. According to the National Coalition for Parent Involvement in Education, the following are the keys to successful parent involvement programs:

- ♦ Assess family's needs and interests about ways of working with the schools.
- ♦ Set clear and measurable objectives based on parent and community input, to help foster a sense of cooperation and communication among families, communities, and schools.
- ♦ Hire and train a parent/family liaison to directly contact parents and coordinate family activities. The liaison should be bilingual as needed and

sensitive to the needs of family and the community, including the non-English-speaking community.

♦ Develop multiple outreach mechanisms to inform families, businesses, and the community about family involvement policies and programs through newsletter, slide shows, videotapes, and local newspapers.

♦ Recognize the importance of a community's historic, ethnic, linguistic, or cultural resources in generating interest in family involvement.

♦ Use creative forms of communication between educators and families that are personal, goal oriented, and make optimal use of new communication technologies.

♦ Mobilize parents/families as volunteers in the school assisting with instructional tasks, meal service, and administrative office functions. Family members might also act as invited classroom speakers and volunteer tutors.

♦ Provide staff development for teachers and administrators to enable them to work effectively with families and with each other as partners in the educational process.

♦ Ensure access to information about nutrition, healthcare, services for individuals with disabilities, and support provided by schools or community agencies.

♦ Schedule programs and activities flexibly to reach diverse family groups.

♦ Evaluate the effectiveness of family involvement programs and activities on a regular basis (http://www.ncpie.org/ncpieguidelines.html).

As you can see from this list, the role of our schools in relation to familial needs has strengthened and increased dramatically. No longer are schools seen as institutions existing solely for the purpose of imparting knowledge to children. Rather, modern schools must meet cultural, social, and educational needs of families as well. This not only requires schools to reach out to parents, but it also behooves them to utilize parents as resources. Not doing so would make the large-scale task schools face larger and, perhaps, insurmountable.

Effectively dealing with our most difficult parents requires us to understand the importance and nature of their involvement. In the school business, whether we are school leaders, teachers, or support staff members, we are dealing with people's most precious commodity—their children. Being mindful of this every time a difficult parent enters our school will help us to at least understand a small piece of where this person is coming from.

16

INCREASING PARENTAL INVOLVEMENT WITH SCHOOL

"For schools to get better, we need more active parents. The more involved parents get in education —their own children's and the nation's—the better our schools will become." (Hirshberg, 1999)

This simple truth begs one very important question. Given what we now know and understand about parental involvement, how do we increase it for the benefit of all of our students? More specifically, what are some methods that schools can use to increase parent involvement and make it productive? These two questions concern schoolteachers and principals all across the country. Regardless of the demographics of any particular school, the notion of parental involvement's value is the same. It does not matter if your school is on the east coast, the west coast, or someplace in between. Whether your school can be classified as rural, urban, or any place in between is completely irrelevant. Simply put, students are more successful in schools that foster cooperation and personal relationships between school personnel and parents. Said another way, "Collaboration is strengthened through weaving the web of personal relationships. Community builders recognize that, as human beings, we need the opportunity to respond to each other, and, just as important, to feel known and seen as valued community contributors" (Brown and Isaacs, 1994, p. 516).

The concept of community and the sense of schools as communities cannot, therefore, be overstated. One of the strengths of American public schools has always been the important role that they have played as centers of the community. Researchers are beginning to point out, however, that feelings of community can no longer be taken for granted. Instead, we have to build community, affirm its values and its membership, and infuse it with the energy, imagination, and commitment of the group (Sterling, 1998). The task of making our schools function as communities lies in the hands of administrators and teachers. The connections that are built when school personnel transform their schools into communities are strong and necessary. As Ruth Charney states,

> In today's world, it is particularly urgent that we extend beyond the domain of self and the lessons of self-control. We need to find connections to others and to feel ourselves members of many groups —intimate group, community groups, and a world group. (Charney, 1992, p. 14)

Allowing parents to believe that they are important members of our school communities is no easy task. Due to a myriad of issues, many of which we have already discussed, a large percentage of our parents simply do not believe that we, as school leaders, deem their involvement to be at all important. Elaine McEwan, educational consultant and author, offers 50 suggestions for getting parental involvement and support started. Included in her list are school climate and school culture issues, such as creating an inviting, welcoming atmosphere and holding regularly scheduled open houses and parent-teacher conferences. These kinds of activities strengthen the feelings of openness and goodwill that are so important. Going further, McEwan suggests structuring school projects, such as fun fairs, so that parents and teachers work together, and hosting career days in which parents "come to school and educate children about their careers" (McEwan, 1998b, pp. 80–89). These structured or forced gatherings of parents and teachers together helps to break down the invisible wall that so many parents feel standing between them and the school. Moreover, when parents can share their careers and/or expertise with children in our schools, their sense of value and worth to our mission and goals is certainly heightened.

Think for a moment of your own positive school activities, which have involved parents in significant ways. In all likelihood you will recall strong feelings of commonality and at least a temporary "breaking down" of barriers between parents and the school. We have both led schools that hosted several fun fairs and field day activities that required parents and teachers to work side by side. The equalization of these two distinct roles that came about as a result of these activities was, in all cases, positive. Parents saw teachers in a new light, and teachers saw a very cooperative, caring side of parents. Perhaps more important, students enjoyed seeing their parents working with their teachers. This was particularly so when the students liked the teacher in question. As part of our own humanity, we all enjoy introducing people that we respect and admire to one another. We can recall many instances in which a respected colleague, supervisor, or teacher was introduced to one of our family members. It brought us great joy to have these two people, whom we admired and respected, meet each other for the first time.

Obviously, an organization that greatly supports parental involvement in our schools is the National PTA. On its Legislative Program Web site, it offers the following position regarding parental involvement:

> When parents are involved, students achieve more, regardless of socioeconomic status, ethnic/racial background or the parents' economic level. The most accurate predictor of a student's achievement in school is not income or social status, but the extent to which the student's family is able to (1) create a home environment that encourages learning; (2) communicate high, yet reasonable, expectations for their children's achievement and future careers; and (3) become involved in their children's education at school and in the community. (http://www.pta.org/programs/legdirect/dir2.htm, 1999)

Understanding the reasons for welcoming and involving parents in your school is only half of the battle. The remainder of the issue is how to go about accomplishing this. In your own experiences, you are probably aware of schools that use innovative, purposeful efforts to increase the involvement of all parents. Sharing all of these programs in this book would be an exhaustive, impossible task. Some of these efforts are unique, serving the special needs of the community in which the school is located. Still others are broader in their appeal. As such, with few modifications, they could be implemented in virtually any school. Below are twenty-seven programs discovered during research conducted by the North Central Regional Educational Laboratory (http://www.ncrel.org/). As Figure 16.1 (pp. 169–174) indicates, these programs differ in their magnitude, target audience, and focus. They share one common factor, though. That is, they increase parental involvement within the schools that implement them.

What these programs have in common is the understanding that schools need parents to assist in their day-to-day operations. Additionally, all of these programs involve an element of appreciation that is shown to the parents. If we, as educators, wish to reduce the frequency and tenacity of our most difficult parent encounters, does it not stand to reason that accomplishing this requires us to show our appreciation to helpful parents? We think it does. Our experience as teachers and principals shows us that nothing improves a person's hearing more than praise. Therefore, praise your parents for all of the ways that they assist you. Do so sincerely. You may be surprised at the reduction of difficult encounters you have with parents once you recognize and implement this.

THE PARENT RESOURCE ROOM

As many schools have discovered, it became apparent to the staff at one of our schools that the parents in the community did not always feel welcome or comfortable in the school. This was unfortunate for so many different reasons. Chief among them was the fact that in this particular community many parents were available during the school day. The unemployment rate was higher than it was insome surround-

(Text continues on page 175.)

FIGURE 16.1 PROGRAMS TO INCREASE PARENTAL INVOLVEMENT

Program	Target Population*	Magnitude of the Program**	Program's Focus			
			Family	Parents	Parents/Teacher Relations	School Services Coordination & Collaboration
AVANCE	P,E	N	Family Literacy	Parent Education; Parental Support; Adult Education		School Services Coordination/Collaboration
Books and Beyond		N	Family Literacy			School Faculty Training
Cooperative Communication Between Home and Family	E,M	N	Information and Advocacy	Information and Advocacy		School Services Coordination/Collaboration; School Faculty Training
Early Intervention for School Success	P,E	S		Parent Education		School Faculty Training

* P = Pre-K; E = Elementary; M = Middle; H = High
** N = National; S = State; D = District/Co.; C = Community; SB = School-based

Program	Target Population*	Magnitude of the Program**	Program's Focus			
			Family	Parents	Parents/ Teacher Relations	School Services Coordination & Collaboration
Families and Schools Together	P,E,M	N		Parental Support	Parent/ Teacher Relations	
Family Math	E	N,SB		Parent Education; Parental Support	Parent/ Teacher Relations	School Faculty Training
Family Outreach Program	P,E,M,H	C	Family Literacy; Home Visiting	Parent Education; Parental Support		School Services Coordination/ Collaboration
Family Study Institute	E,M	S		Parent Education	Parent/ Teacher Relations	School Faculty Training

* P = Pre-K; E = Elementary; M = Middle; H = High

** N = National; S = State; D = District/Co.; C = Community; SB = School-based

Program	Target Population*	Magnitude of the Program**	Program's Focus			
			Family	Parents	Parents/ Teacher Relations	School Services Coordination & Collaboration
FAST Forward	E,M	S				
HIPPY	P	N	Home Visiting	Parent Education		
Learning Center Even Start	P,E,M,H	C	Family Literacy	Parent Volunteers; Parental Support; Adult Education		School Services Coordination/ Collaboration
McAllen Parent Involvement		D	Home Visiting	Parent Education; Parental Support		
MegaSkills	P,E,M	N	Family Literacy	Parent Education; Parental Support	Parent/ Teacher Relations	School Services Coordination/ Collaboration

* P = Pre-K; E = Elementary; M = Middle; H = High
** N = National; S = State; D = District/Co.; C = Community; SB = School-based

Program	Target Population*	Magnitude of the Program**	Program's Focus				
			Family	Parents	Parents/ Teacher Relations	School Services Coordination & Collaboration	
Minnesota Early Childhood/ Family Education	P	S		Parent Education; Parental Support; Parent Volunteers			
NAPE	P,E,M,H	N	Information and Advocacy				
National Coalition for Parent Involvement in Education	P,E,M,H	N	Information and Advocacy				
National PTA	E,M,H	N,SB		Parental Support	Parent/ Teacher Relations		

* P = Pre-K; E = Elementary; M = Middle; H = High
** N = National; S = State; D = District/Co.; C = Community; SB = School-based

Program	Target Population*	Magnitude of the Program**	Program's Focus			
			Family	Parents	Parents/ Teacher Relations	School Services Coordination & Collaboration
PACE	P	S	Family Literacy	Parent Education; Adult Education		
Parent/Child PreSchool	P	SB		Parent Education; Parental Support		
Parent/Child Program	P	D	Family Literacy	Parent Education; Parental Support; Adult Education; Adult Volunteers		
Parents as Educational Partners	P,E,M,H	D	Home Visiting	Parent Volunteers; Parental Support	Parent/ Teacher Relations	School Faculty Training

* P = Pre-K; E = Elementary; M = Middle; H = High
** N = National; S = State; D = District/Co.; C = Community; SB = School-based

Program	Target Population*	Magnitude of the Program**	Program's Focus			
			Family	Parents	Parents/ Teacher Relations	School Services Coordination & Collaboration
Parents as Teachers	P	N		Parent Education; Parental Support		
Partnership 2000 Schools	E,M,H	N,SB		Parent Education		School Faculty Training
PERC	E	D		Parent Education		School Services Coordination/ Collaboration
Project Ahead	E	D		Parent Education		School Services Coordination/ Collaboration

* P = Pre-K; E = Elementary; M = Middle; H = High
** N = National; S = State; D = District/Co.; C = Community; SB = School-based

ing communities, and the traditional values of the community were such that many mothers chose to stay at home during the day. Unlike the situation in many other schools, there was an abundance of resource help, in the form of parents, available to the staff whenever they were needed. However, we must remember that availability is but one necessary component of getting parents involved in a school. More important is the notion that parents need a reason to come to our schools. For many of them, particularly those who have suffered through some of their own negative school experiences, finding a reason is often easier said than done. Hence, the situation exists in many schools that parents are available, but only a select few routinely involve themselves in the school. The staff of this particular school, like many school staffs across America, needed to give parents reasons to be involved in school.

In response to the need for increased parental involvement, the staff at this school decided to create a Parent Resource Room. The goals for this room were simple. First, it needed to be a place where parents could come to get information that would be helpful to them, as parents. Second, the room needed to serve as a place where parents could do work and perform tasks that would be of benefit to students and teachers. Third, and in many ways most important, parents needed to feel some ownership in the room so that it would be a safe and welcoming place within the school in which they could gather.

The room was designed with all three of these goals in mind. One wall of the Parent Resource Room was devoted to parenting materials (pamphlets, books, videos, and games) that the social worker provided. These items were made available for parents to take home with them temporarily, or they could be viewed and examined while the parent stayed in the room. On this side of the room, there was a carpeted area with two rocking chairs for parents to sit in and, it was hoped, feel a sense of comfort. On the opposite wall stood a large shelving unit, on which the staff placed a large bin for each teacher, labeled with his/her name. When teachers found themselves facing those tasks that were difficult for them to find time for but important to their classroom operations, they placed the materials and instructions for completing these tasks inside their bin. Projects that got placed in the bins ranged from simple bulletin board tasks such as cutting out letters, to the creation of art projects, to the development of mathematics flash cards, and beyond. At the base of this wall and extending into the center of the room were two long tables surrounded by chairs.

An important design element of the Parent Resource Room was one blank wall, which parents were encouraged to decorate as they saw fit. In this particular instance, the parents decided to put painted hand prints all over the wall. Selected students representing each grade and class in the school created these. Not only was this appropriate decor for an elementary school, but also the design of it empowered the parents and gave them a real sense of ownership in the room.

It is important to note that the creation of this room did not magically transform parents' attitudes and lead them in flocks to be involved in the school. Over time, however, the results were very close to a flock of parents becoming involved. At first, the same few parents who were always involved spent time in the room. This, in retrospect, was probably to be expected. As the room became better known, a few more got involved. There was a sense of security for some parents in knowing that this room belonged to them. They still needed to stop by the office upon entering the school building, but they were then free to go to *their* resource room. Many of them, to the delight of the school staff, worked for teachers while in the room. Some of them simply sat in the room and visited, slowly but surely building up their level of comfort at being in the school at all.

As word spread of the Parent Resource Room, one of the parent volunteers contacted the local newspaper. As a result of this contact, the school was treated to a full-page story touting the room's benefits. This, along with the praises being sung by the teachers who benefitted from the parents' efforts, made the room a very popular site in the school building. Not only were the three original goals accomplished, but there were many other benefits, as well. These included:

- There was at least one small corner of the school in which all parents felt welcome.

- Students of this community, for the first time, got very used to parents being in the building. This helped create a bond between school and home.

- Teachers began to see parents as very helpful and much less threatening and critical than they had once perceived them to be.

- Parents knew what went on in the school building on a regular basis. While they were not roaming the halls, due to the distraction that this would cause for students' learning, they were in the building. They could experience the climate on a regular basis.

- Most significant, for the first time in many of their lives, the parents were a valuable, integral part of the school's culture. (Fiore, 2001, p. 89)

The staff at this school, we must note, were very fortunate to have a vacant room in their school for the creation of a Parent Resource Room. This, obviously, is not a luxury all schools enjoy. This, then, is one of the challenges facing many educators today. In the absence of space, can they make parents feel more welcome in their school? Can they provide resources that are helpful to parents, while expecting nothing in return? Can they include parents in a way that makes them feel as if the school is partly their school?

The answer is a resounding "Yes" if educators will first accept the responsibility for involving parents. Though the creation of a Parent Resource Room is not always possible, a commitment to recognizing the worth of parents and giving them a place in school decisions will accomplish the same mission. It is the understanding of the valuable role parents play in their children's education that is sorely needed. This understanding must rest with the principal and the teachers if it is to have any hope of being universally accepted by the school community.

OBSTACLES TO INVOLVING
PARENTS AT SCHOOL

We must recognize that there are several structural difficulties inherent in some school environments that pose additional challenges to keeping parents involved. One is the size of the school. Without question, parents of children who attend very large schools often feel more intimidated by the school than do parents of children in smaller schools. There is also a tendency in larger schools for parents to feel as if they are lost in the shuffle. While these issues are real, and do affect some of our parents, they are not reasons to give up and conclude that larger schools cannot enjoy opportunities for strong parental involvement. In fact, many of the previously described programs have been successfully implemented in rather large schools. What is required is an understanding that larger schools can seem intimidating to parents. With this understanding will come a desire to look for ways to effectively "shrink" the school for many parents. Breaking it up into smaller units (i.e., having a parent association for each grade level) is one way that school leaders have found for overcoming this structural difficulty. For example, even very large high schools often have powerful parent booster clubs where such clubs are focused more narrowly on certain extracurricular areas and do not try to be representative of the entire high school community.

Another way in which some schools have chosen to address this obstacle is by implementing a "school within a school" philosophy. Larger schools are broken down into smaller units along such lines as grade levels or subject areas. Each of these smaller units is considered in many ways to be a separate school. The concept is similar to one that has been employed by larger universities for years. In these institutions, academic units are broken down into colleges or schools. Again, what is required by educators is an understanding that size can be an important structural barrier that many parents find intimidating.

GUILTY UNTIL PROVEN INNOCENT?

Furthermore, we often alienate parents by our safety structures, which effectively make visitors feel unwelcome. As previously stated, we want and need our schools to be safe. Equally important, we want our parents to perceive our schools as being the safest possible places for them to send their children. Announcing your commitment to school safety as soon as a visitor enters the building is, therefore, an excellent idea. How you choose to announce it is another matter altogether. Think back to the points in Chapter 6 about the welcoming greeting that meets parents when they arrive at your school's doors. The importance of greeting all visitors with a friendly, welcoming statement cannot be overstated. As educators concerned with cultivating positive parental relationships, we must ensure that the guiding message behind all of our interactions with parents is, "We're glad you're here." Anything less than that contributes, though often unintentionally, to the negative feelings that some of our parents have. We are all for increased safety measures designed to keep students secure while they are at school. What we have difficulty understanding is unfriendly methods for employing increased safety. Let's not make parents feel as though they are guilty of wrongdoing the moment they enter our school.

A related concern involves the use of "badges" that visitors wear when they are in school buildings. In a nutshell, the purpose of these badges is to identify the visitor and/or show individuals who are in regular attendance (i.e., students and staff) that this visitor has, in fact, already reported to the office. We have both been in schools where only some of the visitors were wearing these badges. For the most part, these visitors fell into one of two categories. Either they were (a) individuals who rarely visited the school and would not be recognized by many people, or (b) highly recognized people who habitually follow rules. Other visitors, typically those who were often in the school and were known by virtually everybody, wandered around without having first picked up a badge in the office. In many cases, rather than risk insulting these people by confronting them, staff members in these schools allowed the visitors to be in the school without badges. This is unfair and upsetting to many parents. Consider the message we are giving visitors when we only require some of them to wear visitors badges. Though not necessarily intentional, we are saying that highly recognized visitors hold status different from those who only visit us occasionally. Either everybody should wear a visitor's badge or nobody should. Today, with the safety concerns our schools have, the best answer is for everybody to wear them.

As educators, we need to rethink parental involvement. We need to be creative in welcoming parents to school, and we must provide opportunities to help them to be involved at school. In doing so, however, we cannot confuse involvement with support. Many parents are supportive of our efforts, but cannot be involved. At least, they don't think they can be involved because we haven't helped them to rethink what involvement means. While this chapter has provided some ideas for rethinking involvement at school, as Chapter 17 illustrates, support from home can sometimes be even more important.

17

INCREASING PARENTAL INVOLVEMENT AT HOME

Too many people equate parental involvement with parents physically coming to the school building and volunteering. This is largely due to the reluctance of some schools to view parental roles in relation to education differently than they previously had. The seeming unwillingness to acknowledge or embrace change has forced many educators to view parental involvement from this narrow perspective. Though some aspects of schooling (i.e., technology, pedagogical knowledge, and scheduling) have undergone admirable transformations in recent years, the understanding that parents of today are different than those we may have grown accustomed to has been ignored in many schools. Given the statistics reviewed earlier regarding the percentage of parents unavailable during school hours, it appears obvious that schools must consider other ways to get and to keep parents involved. Add to this our knowledge regarding parental feelings of fear and intimidation at the mere mention of going to their child's school, and it becomes clear that we must discover new and better ways to involve parents from within their own homes. As Philip Schlechty states, "More and more children from affluent homes as well as from poor families, do not come from environments that reflect Dick and Jane, Mother and Father, Spot and Puff." (Schlechty, 1997, p. 236) Educators must recognize this.

COMMUNICATION IS THE KEY

There are numerous ways in which schools can keep parents involved in their children's education while respecting the fact that many of them are unable or unwilling to physically come to the school. An obvious first step is for the school to regularly communicate with parents. The caveat to remember here is that the best communication is two-way. That is, giving and receiving information are equally important. Many superintendents, principals, and teachers fail in this regard because they mistakenly believe that sending home regular newsletters and following up on phone calls constitutes effective communication. Though those things are important, they are simply not enough. The best educators provide opportunities to listen to the concerns of others. As far as parents are concerned, these educators create numerous opportunities for parents to do the talking. They do such things as host socials in which parents come to school and collectively speak with the principal. They place suggestion boxes in accessible places so that parents who are unwilling to initially speak face to face with school officials can still have their concerns heard. They do these things, as well as other more innovative things, to increase the amount of time spent listening. Fundamental to all human relations or communications training is the concept that people often wish to be heard before they are willing to listen. School leaders, as well as every other educational employee, must begin understanding that parents who feel listened to will be much more likely to listen to and trust you.

Though educators have been hearing about the benefits of regular, purposeful communication with parents for years, it is important for teachers and administrators to know that parents are also receiving the same information. The National Coalition for Parent Involvement in Education (NCPIE), one of the larger and more influential parent advocacy groups, says that schools should regularly communicate with parents about their child's progress and the educational objectives of the school. Furthermore, this organization strongly encourages parents who are not receiving such information to ask for it. Again, the concept of two-way communication is alluded to. This coalition, along with the National Committee for Citizens in Education, is fulfilling a niche that parents never used to ask for and did not consequently appear to need. Specifically, they are counseling parents about how to get involved in their children's education. In many ways, these organizations are making the school personnel's jobs easier. By offering the following suggestions to parents, these organizations are informing parents that they must actively seek involvement in their children's school. Furthermore, they are making the important point that parents can be partners in schooling from within the confines of their own homes. Not only is that a welcome idea for some parents, but also it validates the fact that family needs have certainly changed over time. The National Committee for Citizens in Education urges all parents to:

+ Support student events and performances by helping with them (such as sewing costumes or planning scenery for a school play).

+ Be part of decision-making committees dealing with school issues and problems, such as a Parent Advisory Committee (these often meet during the evening).

+ Ask your child's teacher if he or she has materials that you can use to help your child at home.

+ Help your child develop a homework schedule that he or she can stick to.

+ Have high expectations for your child's learning and behavior, both at home and at school.

+ Avoid making homework a punishment.

+ Praise and encourage your child.

This is also a welcome relief to school personnel, for it acknowledges that successful parent-school partnerships involve efforts from both parties. It is absolutely true that school personnel must reach out to and involve more parents. It is also true that parents must take an active role in their children's education, regardless of whether the school appears to be inviting them. This is often where the conflict begins. Parents feel that the school does not welcome them, while the school personnel feel that parents are unwilling to help or be supportive. The bottom line, though, a point that has been expanded upon in several previous chapters, is that effective communication is a key in dealing with difficult parents.

Some individual school districts have taken the initiative to inform parents of ways in which they can be involved with school from within their homes. Stephen Kleinsmith, assistant superintendent in Millard, Nebraska, encourages faculty and staff to share the following list of parent involvement options with parents:

♦ Call the school staff on a regular basis, and talk with teachers before problems occur.

♦ Help proofread and edit the school newsletter.

♦ Become involved in the student's curriculum planning, and discuss academic options with your son or daughter.

♦ Encourage involvement in the school activities of the student's choice.

♦ Ask your son or daughter, "What good questions did you ask today?" or "What did you learn in school today?" Then practice good listening, a key to effective communication.

♦ Encourage reading, using the library, and purchasing books at a young age. (Dietz, 1997)

Though not exhaustive, these suggestions can form the foundation of any school's efforts at increasing parental involvement. Essentially, all that is required is for educators to recognize the value of parental involvement in a child's education. Then, an understanding that parents and the situations they find themselves in are much different than they once appeared to be must develop. Finally, educators must communicate to parents that there are ways in which they can be involved without ever having to come to school during regular school hours.

This information can also be understood by looking at Figure 17.1. As this figure illustrates, parents can be examined on two separate continuums. On the one hand, we can consider the degree to which the parent supports the child. As we know from our experiences, parents can be neglectful in the worst case to encouraging in the best.

On the other hand, we need to examine the degree to which the parent is involved in school activities. Again, this involvement can occur at school or at home. As we all know, there are parents who are completely uninvolved with school, and there are parents who are involved.

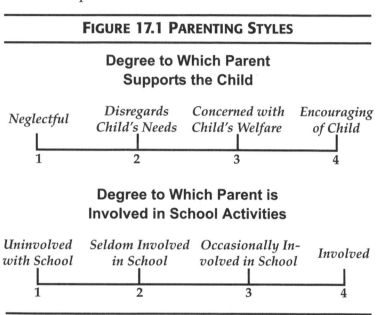

FIGURE 17.1 PARENTING STYLES

**Degree to Which Parent
Supports the Child**

Neglectful	Disregards Child's Needs	Concerned with Child's Welfare	Encouraging of Child
1	2	3	4

**Degree to Which Parent is
Involved in School Activities**

Uninvolved with School	Seldom Involved in School	Occasionally Involved in School	Involved
1	2	3	4

The best case scenario would be if all parents were rated a 4 on both of these scales. However, a parent who scores low on the school involvement scale but high on the child support scale is a parent who must be helped to recognize the important role that they play. Being supportive of their child and the activities that the child engages in at school is vitally important to that child's success. When this support is combined with involvement in school activities, then children are more likely to succeed.

SUCCESS STORIES FROM AROUND THE COUNTRY

There is a multitude of success stories wherein local schools have developed innovative ways to involve parents who are otherwise unable to come to the school and assist in traditional manners. In addition to the important task of creating positive learning environments at home and speaking positively about school, parents in many school communities are asked to supplement their children's learning at home. Epstein and associates (Epstein, 1992), for example, have developed a program called Teachers Involve Parents in Schoolwork (TIPS) that helps teachers to adapt materials for home learning in several curricular areas. Central to the program is the idea that TIPS homework assignments must have student-family interaction built in to all assignments. Evaluations of the program's effectiveness have consistently produced positive results. Among initial findings, program researchers discovered that large numbers of parents, previously not involved with their children's homework, were actively involved in TIPS; teachers were reporting much higher rates of return for TIPS homework than for regular homework; and the TIPS program itself helped teachers communicate with parents.

The Parent Partnership program in Philadelphia, another example of an innovation involving parental involvement from home, provides reading and mathematics booklets to parents as well as a Dial-A-Teacher Assistance project for help with homework in all basic subjects. Many school systems in recent years have expanded on the Dial-A-Teacher concept to include help and assignment information via the Internet. Also, used in some markets is local access cable television. These telecasts can include advice for parents on providing assistance, as well as the more traditional call-in help programs for students.

The San Diego Unified School District offers materials in both English and Spanish designed to assist in student homework. This is in recognition of the fact that many students do not live in homes that use English as the typical language for communication. As a result, many parents are not involved in their child's school because of an honest barrier to communication. As educators, we sometimes mistakenly assume that parents have the same command of English as the children we work with do. Often, we have discovered, this is not the case.

As in San Diego, many school districts are providing information to parents in multiple languages to reduce this obvious barrier to parental involvement.

Finally, many special education programs across the country have long been involving parents in supplementing their children's learning at home (Turnbull and Turnbull, 1990). Beginning back in the days when parents of special needs students were responsible for much of their child's education, this movement grew out of necessity. Today, when parents are much more aware of the local school's responsibility to educate all children, we still see the leftover by-product of increased parental involvement with students receiving special services.

In addition to assisting schools by supplementing the curriculum, parents are asked to assist in other tasks vital to the success of school programs. At Parkview Elementary School in Valparaiso, Indiana, for example, parents are instrumental in creating the school's annual overnight reading program, Friday Night Live. This program, which temporarily transforms Parkview into a new themed environment each year, is designed to assist children in the association of reading with fun. The school, which has been transformed into an Olympic Village, Hollywood, a beach, a hotel, and a railroad, relies heavily on parental support to accomplish the goals of this program. Though many of Parkview's parents do assist at the school, Friday Night Live requires several months of labor to be completed at home, out of the students' sight. Parents sew, build giant structures out of wood, paint, cook, and plan for the event from their homes, during the hours they have available outside of their workdays. Their reward is the delight of students when the big day arrives and the secret theme is revealed. This involvement is as instrumental to student success as involvement that requires parents to be present at school during the academic day. However, it respects the fact that such involvement is not always possible. This, in turn, does a great deal toward strengthening the relationship between parents and school staff at this particular school.

Hopefully, you too can think of ways in which your own school utilizes parent volunteers without requiring them to assist at the school during the school day. If not, we encourage you to make the effort to reach out to and involve parents in this way. This will lead to a decrease in the number of difficult parents you encounter, as more of them will begin to recognize their importance on your team. Disagreements with teammates are far less volatile than are disagreements between members of opposing teams. Making parents believe that they are your teammates is an important first step in reducing the number of difficult ones you are required to deal with.

IT'S THE SIMPLE THINGS YOU DO

Keep in mind, though, that parental involvement extends beyond projects that are completed at home. Parents are involved at home every time they take an active role in their child's studies. This key point must be shared with parents on a regular basis. The importance of strong communication skills in dealing with difficult parents has been further elaborated on throughout this book. Informing parents of their importance in reading to their children, monitoring their homework, and discussing expectations regarding conduct and citizenship are among the most significant ways that schools can involve parents at home. Remember, as we have said, to share this information with parents. Repeat it as many times as is necessary. Again, if I recognize and really believe that you consider me to be important, am I more likely or less likely to be difficult in dealings with you? We think the answer is obvious.

Finally, it is so important to remember that there are specific parenting practices that empirical data has shown are related to students' academic achievement. In fact, according to some researchers, there is an even greater link between student achievement and parental engagement at home than there is between student achievement and parental engagement at school (Finn, 1998: Wang et al., 1993).

Broadly defined, the three types of parental support at home that have most consistently been linked with increased school performance are:

- Actively organizing and monitoring the child's time
- Helping with homework
- Discussing school matters with the child (Finn, 1998)

Though the form that these activities take will certainly differ somewhat from family to family, it is vitally important for educators to consistently affirm their value. We must stop making parents feel guilty for not being involved with their children at school. At the same time, every one of us needs to inform parents that the above-mentioned activities greatly increase the chances that their children will be successful in school. Parents who recognize this should be celebrated and made to feel like they are valuable members of the school community.

PARTING
THOUGHTS

If our goal has been accomplished, you have generated some new resources to use with the most challenging of parents or the most trying of situations. If we always keep in mind the critical elements of working hard to get parents on our side, then many times we will face less challenging people and hopefully even soften the difficult situations. Effectively communicating when we do face these times is essential. Remembering to always be professional and do our best in seeming calm and yet confident can help stem even the highest of tides.

Even those of us who do establish ties to parents also need additional items in our bag of tricks that we can rely on in times of need. Hopefully this book has provided some additional tools that all educators can rely on in supporting their essential mission of educating every student to the best of our ability. Always remember that the more challenging the parents are, the more their child needs us to be the voice of reason and to always model the way a person *should* act rather than reflect the way they *do* act.

Remember that no one likes to deal with these parents (unfortunately including their children), but, the good people do it anyhow.

REFERENCES

Benson, C., Buckley, S., & Elliott, A. (1980). Families as educators: Time use contributions to school achievement. In J. Gutherie (Ed.), *School Finance Policy in the 1980s*. Cambridge, MA: Ballinger.

Bissell, B. (1992, July). The paradoxical leader. Paper presented at the Missouri Leadership Academy, Columbia, MO.

Blankenhorn, D. (1995). Pay, papa, pay. *National Review, 47*(6), 34–42.

Brown, J., & Isaacs, D. (1994). *The Fifth Discipline Fieldbook: Strategies and Tools for Building a Learning Organization*. Garden City, NY: Doubleday.

Charney, R. (1992). *Teaching Children to Care: Management in the Responsive Classroom*. Greenfield, MA: The Northeast Foundation for Children.

Comer, J. (1998). *Waiting for a Miracle: Why Schools Can't Solve Our Problems—And How We Can*. New York: Dutton/Plum.

Connecticut Department of Social Services. (1999). Online source: www.dss.state.ct.us

Covey, Stephen R. (1990). *The Seven Habits of Highly Effective People Restoring the Character Ethic*. New York: Simon & Schuster.

Data on Homeless Children and Youth (1999). Online source: www.serve.org/nche/SEASdata.htm.

Dietz, Michael J. (1997). *School, Family, and Community: Techniques and Models for Successful Collaboration*. Gaithersburg, MD: Aspen Publishers.

Epstein, J. (1992). Schools reaching out increase family community involvement. *Report: Current Research and Development, 1*, p. 15. Baltimore, MD: Center on Families, Communities, Schools, and Children Learning, John Hopkins University.

Epstein, J. L. (1995). School/family/community partnerships: Caring for the children we share. *Phi Delta Kappan, 76*(9), 701–712.

Finn, Jeremy D. (1998). Parental engagement that makes a difference. *Educational Leadership, 55*(8), 20–24.

Fiore, Douglas J. (2001). *Creating Connections for Better Schools.* Larchmont, NY: Eye on Education.

Galley, Michelle. (2000). Chicago to size up parents with "checklists." *Education Week, 11*(8): 3.

Goals 2000 (1995). *The National Education Goals Report 1995.* Washington, DC: Government Printing Office.

Hirshberg, C. (1999, September). How good are our schools? *Life.*

Lightfoot, S. (1978). *Worlds Apart: Relationships between Families and Schools.* New York: Basic Books.

McEwan, Elaine K. (1998a). *Angry Parents, Failing Schools: What's Wrong with the Public Schools & What You Can Do about It.* Cincinnati, OH: Harold Shaw.

McEwan, Elaine K. (1998b). *How to Deal with Parents Who Are Angry, Troubled, Afraid or Just Plain Crazy.* Thousand Oaks, CA: Corwin Press.

National Association of Elementary School Principals. (1993). *Newsletter Do's and Don't's.* Reston, VA: Author.

National Association of Secondary School Principals. (1996). *Breaking Ranks: Changing an American Institution.* Reston, VA: Author.

National Data Book. (1998). *Statistical Abstract of the United States, 118th Edition.* Baton Rouge, LA: Claitors.

National PTA Survey. (1992) Online source: www.ncpie.org/ncpieguidelines.html.

National PTA Legislative Program 1999–2000. (1999). Online source: www.pta.org/programs/legdirect/dir2.htm.

North Central Regional Educational Laboratory. (1999). Online source: www.ncrel.org.

Phillips, G. (1997, November). Paper presented at the Indiana Principal Leadership Academy, Indianapolis, IN.

Procidano, Mary E. & Fisher, Celia B. (1992). *Contemporary Families: A Handbook for School Professionals*. New York: Teachers College Press.

Rioux, J. William, & Berla, Nancy. (1993). *Innovations in Parent and Family Involvement*. Larchmont, NY: Eye on Education.

Sarason, S. B. (1995). *Parental Involvement and the Political Principle: Why the Existing Governance Structure of School Should Be Abolished*. San Francisco, CA: Jossey-Bass.

Schlechty, Philip. (1997). *Inventing Better Schools: An Action Plan for Educational Reform*. San Francisco, CA: Jossey-Bass.

Shinn, Marybeth & Weitzman, Beth C. (1990) Research on Homelessness: An introduction. *Journal of Social Issues* 46(4): 1–11.

Steinberg, L. (1997). *Beyond the Classroom: Why School Reform Has Failed and What Parents Need to Do*. New York: Simon & Schuster.

Sterling, M. (1998). Building a community week by week. *Educational Leadership* 56(1):65–68.

Strickland, G. (1998). *Bad Teachers: The Essential Guide for Concerned Parents*. New York: Pocket Books.

Turnbull, A., & Turnbull, H. (1990). *Families, Professionals, and Exceptionality: A Special Partnership*. Columbus, OH: Merrill.

U.S. Bureau of the Census. (1999). Online source: www.census.gov.

U.S. Bureau of Labor Statistics. (1987). Online source: http://stats.bls.gov.

U.S. Conference of Mayors. (1998). Online source: www.usmayors.org.

U.S. Department of Education. (1997). *Achieving the Goals*. Washington, DC.

Vissing, Yvonne M. (1996). *Out of Sight, Out of Mind: Homeless Children and Families in Small-Town America*. Lexington, KY: University of Kentucky Press.

Wang, M. C., et al. (1993). Toward a knowledge base for school learning. *Review Of Educational Research, 63,* 249–294.

Web Sties for Student Achievement. (1999). Online source: www.naesp.org/students/sslinks.htm.

Williams, David L. Jr., & Chavkin, Nancy Feyl. (1989). Essential elements of strong parent involvement programs. *Educational Leadership, 47*(2), 18–20.

Yao, E. (1988). Working effectively with asian immigrant parents. *Phi Delta Kappan, 70*(3), 223–225.

If you would like information about inviting Todd Whitaker to speak to your group, please contact him at t-whitaker@indstate.edu or his Web site www.toddwhitaker.com